NEXT EXIT, CLARITY

A memoir of childhood trauma, anxiety, healing and finding one's voice.

Heather Rohleder

ISBN:
9798338019580
9798330423941

Book Photo Cover by Heather Rohleder

First Edition November 2024

This book is dedicated to two beautiful souls who taught me to not silence my dreams and reach for the farthest goals possible. Judith Johnson and Opal Johnson. You two are my reason and my why for this book.

Thank you! I love you!

**** Trigger Warning ****

This book talks about trauma, abuse, bullying, eating disorders/body dysphoria, anxiety, depression and death/grief.

Contents

Introduction

Breaking the generational cycle has been such a beautiful yet devastating job. Yes, healing is a full time job. I'm not just a childcare professional and caregiver for the special needs, I'm also a self healer. I'm the first in my family to do the work. First generation if you will.

That moment my body went into this very dark place, I knew I had to do something. This was not at all who I was or who I was meant to be. I've seen first hand what it can do to someone, that someone was and is not me. Healing has been such a beautiful yet messy ride. A ride I don't plan on getting off anytime soon. I've actually mastered so much. Drove down some pretty epic roads if I must say. I've also driven down some very bumpy roads as well. Roads that construct trauma and grief. Anxiety and depression being bystanders along the way. Or as I'd like to say, runaway hitchhikers who jump in the back of the vehicle.

Healing doesn't happen overnight. It is not linear. Does not have a time frame. Healing opens up a lot of wounds. Traumatic wounds as I'd like to call them. Trauma is not linear as well. Trauma takes time to process. Takes time to understand. To accept. It does not go away. Trauma is a life long partner who will randomly show up when triggered by the past. When we start putting bandaids on these wounds, a lot of emotions come into play. Grief being one of them.

Grieving what was is complete validation of the healing process. We're grieving the old version of who we were. We're grieving what was. And that's completely valid. Grief is a little word with so much meaning. Different meanings at that. Grief does not have a time frame just like healing and trauma. It is a life long partner who randomly shows up when it's been triggered by so many different things and people.

I'm pretty sure I've had anxiety since childhood yet not being diagnosed til my early 30s. Healing is a trigger to the nervous system. Traumatic events are a huge trigger to the nervous system. When the nervous system is triggered, anxiety comes out to play. It either protects us from what's happening/about to happen or it can full on make the situation worse than what it really is. My anxiety for the most part tries to control the uncontrolled. Sits with the "what ifs." Allows the "worst case scenarios" to come tag along for play time. Since starting this healing journey, my anxiety has been at its highest but with all the research I've done and tools I've been given, I know what needs to happen in order to calm the nerves. To push anxiety away.

Since being on this healing journey and taking care of my trauma, I've finally found something that was taken from me at such a young age. It's been found a few times while growing up but then it'd get ripped away faster than I can reach for it. I have finally found my voice. At the age of 38, I've finally found my voice to speak my truth. Crazy, huh?

I'm here to let those of you who are still battling to find yours to not give up! You WILL get it back. I'm here to tell you that your truth WILL be told. And when it is, nobody can take that away from you! It is yours forever!

1

CHAPTER

As a child, I was the "shy" girl. The "good girl". The one my parents didn't "have to worry about." The girl who did no harm to others. Put others' needs and emotions before her own. The girl who would follow the crowd, never the leader. I was the "yes ma'am, no sir" child. Respect my elders. Did as I was told. I was also the girl who loved the outdoors. I loved recess. Swinging on swings was my favorite. It's as if I was free from everything and everyone. Never wanted to stay inside. If I was inside, it's because I had to for obvious reasons. Outside with my sister, Jennifer and the neighborhood kids was where I spent most of my days. That's where I met my now best friend of 20+ years, Malerie. Outside was my free zone. My escape from arguments amongst my parents during the night.

Mom had to fight us to come in when the porch lights came on. Those nights would cause friction amongst mom and dad. Dad wanted us in while mom would sometimes cave in and let us stay out another few more minutes. My parents could never agree on parenting. Dad being the "whatever" parent while mom being the one who was constantly punishing us yet letting things slide due to being overwhelmed. There would be times dad would step in yet it'd be towards my mom and not to us, the ones who are causing the mess. I'm pretty sure I'm still grounded till this day due to mom "grounding" us yet letting us go play due to driving her crazy.

Growing up, my parents' relationship with my sister and I was different. There was structure yet there was freedom. We'd have set rules yet we'd be able to do whatever we wanted. That also caused friction in the house during the evenings. Jennifer and I joke that we basically raised ourselves. Our parents were just there. It'd be very rare we would get disciplined for whatever reason. If mom punished us, dad didn't care or if dad punished us, mom didn't agree with it nor care. So, I honestly think, they gave up as we got a lil older and more independent. Let us learn "the hard way." And, if we're being honest, that was probably a good idea. We saw what trouble looked like from those around us. Family and friends. We learned what NOT to do from those certain individuals. We saw the consequences first hand. Mom will tell you today that she didn't have to worry about us growing up. But in reality, she should have. She should have shown us some guidance. Some reassurance. Just because Jennifer and myself knew right from wrong, didn't mean we weren't looking for that guidance and reassurance that we give one another now as adults.

When we're kids, we don't know why our parents did what they did but once we're adults, the light is turned on and we realize the "Why." My mother was fighting her own demons during my childhood while dad was keeping his hidden and stayed busy with work. Even on weekends he was working. Hardly home. When he was settled at home, he stayed distant with us girls until we had to do something as a family. Either it be holidays or just random family trips or spontaneous events. He for the most part kept his distance. As I got older, I realized why. He was exhausted from working all day. Dealing with his own demons. He needed to breathe. Decompose from that day's emotions and what not.

Emotions weren't positively shared amongst us growing up. The "love yous" weren't shared frequently amongst our parents. Towards one another and towards us girls. We weren't a hugging type family. Why I think I'm such a hugger now. Took me a while to accept hugs, but I'm a pro today. Haha. If we did share our emotions, they'd be silenced with "you're fine." "Get over it." "I'll give you something to cry about." Only because, again, our parents didn't know how to regulate their own emotions. Didn't know how to understand others' emotions. Parents were emotionally immature. Emotionally unavailable. We'd be consoled yet we'd be turned away depending on the severity of why we were reacting in such a way. Growing up in a household where emotions were invalid, it set me up for failure as an adult.

Not knowing how to control/regulate my own emotions. Understand my behavior. Being scared to voice my concerns. Not knowing how to handle and comfort my own self due to not being shown amongst my parents. It took me quite some time to learn how to regulate and understand my emotions today. Understand my nervous system. Therapy has had such a huge impact in that department for me today.

As I entered school, I became this little girl who was looking for comfort and acceptance from her teachers. I was looking for validation. I was this quiet little girl who kept to herself and hardly had friends. When I did make friends, they'd shum me away the next day as if I didn't exist.

From grade 2 til grade 6, I fought with my mom every day to go to school. We even had to have the school counselors come to my house. It was bad. My grandmother, Judy, even had to come to the house some days. It was a hot mess. Caused friction in the house in the evenings. Mom letting me stay home due to giving up the fight yet dad getting upset that I missed yet another day of school. He'd even yell at me for causing trouble in the house for mom. Looking back now as an adult, my separation anxiety was real. Not wanting to leave my mom. Hoping for that one on one attention that I never got from her when we all were together. When my sister was home.

Growing up, she "favored" my older sister more than me. My dad "favored" me. I was "Daddy's little girl" according to my family. If I wanted anything, dad got it for me. If mom or sister wanted anything from dad, they'd have me ask knowing he'd cave in and get it. So, my relationship with my mother wasn't perfect by any means. Why when I saw the chance to be alone with her, I took it. Even if I knew it'd cause some friction amongst my parents and some days with Jennifer.

Once I entered 5th grade, that's when everything changed for me. I was the new kid. New school. New faces to get to know. New teachers. New everything. It was hard saying I came from a school where everyone knew everyone. Including the school officials. This school had no idea who I was. It was scary. I was befriended by someone who would be in my life up into adulthood. She took it upon herself to show me the ropes of that school. She took it upon herself to play with me at recess. We quickly became best friends.

In the middle of that school year, there was this group of girls that did not like me for whatever reason. They took it upon themselves to start bullying me. They'd call me names at recess. They'd say rude comments in class. Just being nasty. There was one incident during transition time from recess to going back into class, where one of the girls patted me on the back to say "hello." Me, not realizing that as she's patting me on the back, she's also putting glue on the back of my black sweater. She had put glue on her hand and left a handprint on my sweater. Later during the day, a friend came up to me and told me that I have glue on my sweater. I was confused as to what she was talking about. As I turned the sweater around, sure enough, I had glue on my sweater in the form of a handprint. Grass was on it as well. Once I saw the glue and grass, I felt this uneasy feeling start to bubble in my stomach. I felt my face get flushed red. My throat was getting all scratchy as if a lump was forming and I was about to cry. I look around and those girls who did it earlier are chuckling amongst themselves and pointing at me. To say I was hurt and humiliated would be an understatement. Later that day, when I got home, I had hesitated to tell my mom what had happened due to her not doing anything nor believing me. When I did tell my mom what had happened. She told me she'd take care of it and for me to let the teacher know as well. "Everything will be fine" was constantly told to me. The rest of my 5th grade school year was me either playing at recess by myself or staying in the classroom with my teacher playing on the computer or coloring in my notebook.

I am now in 6th grade. New school year. Same girls in my class. Same situation amongst those girls. Name calling at recess. Rude comments in class. This school year I took it amongst myself to try to stick up for myself. Show them that I am not the new girl anymore. I felt empowered to stand up to them. Until I didn't. There would be incidents that took every ounce of energy from me where I had to excuse myself and go to the bathroom and cry. It was too much for me. I'd let my teacher know what was going on. She'd separate the girls from me during class time.

This one incident is what embarrassed me the most. This incident happened during our "Read A Thon." If you're not familiar with what that is, it's when you'd spend all day just reading books that were allowed from home. We were also allowed to bring in a blanket and pillow with some snacks. I remember I brought in a bag of chips and a Sprite. I had asked the teacher if I could go use the restroom. While I was gone, the girls took it upon themselves to go through my backpack and take my stuff, including my snacks. When I came back, I had seen them pointing at me chuckling. I was confused at first as to why they were laughing at me. I then saw my snacks on their desk. That's when it clicked on why they were chuckling at me. I felt this rage form inside of me. Anger building up. I had told the teacher what the girls had done while I went to the restroom. I remember these exact words she had told me, "how do I know the snacks are not theirs and you're just lying to me?" I tried telling her they were mine yet she didn't believe me. I was hurting inside. I felt my stomach drop and a hard pit in my throat. I asked for another bathroom break. I ran to the bathroom and cried in the bathroom stall. Before going back into the classroom, I splashed my face with some cold water so it didn't look as if I was defeated.

Weeks go by and the girls are still bullying me. Verbally attacking me. I'd keep reporting it to my teacher yet nothing was being done. I'd share here and there with my mom of what was happening. All I was told is, "I'll take care of it and everything will be fine." It was the day before the last day of school when this incident that drove my mom to go to the school officials happened.

It was as the bell rang for school to be out for the day. My best friend at the time wanted to get our yearbooks signed by some friends before heading home. I said sure, I'll help. As we're gathering friends' signatures, I feel this hard thing hit my head then hit my back. As I go to touch my head, I feel the rough sharp shells of an egg. I also feel the cold slimy yolk on my head. As I pull my hand off my head and look at it, I can hear my best friend laugh and say that I just got hit with eggs. As she's laughing, I feel this sensation in my body of discomfort & humiliation. I felt my face get all hot and my eyes start to water. As I'm looking around with egg all over my head, back and hands, I see the girls who've been harassing me for the past 2 yrs run off laughing. Kind of like in a movie. That's what it felt like. Till this day, I honestly believe I had an out of body experience. When I got home, I told my mother what had happened. She immediately got on the phone to the school officials. I had never seen her get off the couch so fast and go in full "mom mode." Again, our emotions weren't fully accepted growing up, so this was something new for me to witness. The school had no idea this type of bullying was going on and that they'd take care of it. Needless to say, I missed the last day of school due to my mom not wanting me to possibly go through more trouble. And the school did absolutely nothing about it, due to it being so close to the end of the school year.

I remember that was the longest summer break for me. Dreading the new school year and yet another new school. I didn't want to go back to school. I didn't want to start Jr. High. I was scared of having those girls in my classes. Seeing their faces again. Repeating the last 2 yrs over again. Come to find out, it wouldn't be those girls yet it'd be different people, including family members at some point.

Throughout 7th and 8th grade, I'd be bullied for being too skinny. Being flat chested. Acne was my arch nemesis all through junior high. I would break out so bad, I would be called "pizza sauce face." People would spread rumors about how I throw up my food after lunch or I don't eat anything at all. Why I'm so skinny. I was being labeled as anorexic. I knew the truth, so I wouldn't let it get to me most days. Once my family was aware and starting to believe the rumors, I completely shut down. I would even keep my emotions silent. Trying to explain to them it was false was like trying to teach a lil kid to tie their shoes. It wasn't registering right away. I was watched at family gatherings. Members would ask if I had enough food on my plate. They even would tell me that I needed to eat more and what not. It was too much for me at the time. I'd find myself hiding out in my grandmother's room/bathroom crying. Feeling unheard. Feeling hurt.

To this day, I still have issues with body dysphoria. Getting that self love and self confidence back has been the hardest thus far. Looking in a mirror was the hardest thing throughout my teenage years. Even into adulthood. I'm always thinking about how much I eat and what I eat. If I do get seconds, my family's voices come into my head. If clothes start to "not fit", I start telling myself I need to lose weight. Even on dates as an adult, I'd get asked if I'm the "salad and water" type of girl due to being skinny. If I'd go to the bathroom right after I'm done eating, I would get asked if I just threw the food up. It got to the point where I would not call or text the person back.

Those years of my young adulthood were pretty challenging. Trying to speak my truth yet it wasn't accepted. Trying to raise my voice for them to understand my discomfort yet getting ignored by their own comfort.

Sharing my story of bullying has been a blessing in disguise. It's given me the courage to go back and talk with that version of myself and heal that version. As you will read later in this book. It's allowed me to be the voice for the shaken. It's allowed me to speak up for the survivors of bullying. No matter what "type" of bullying it involves, we are not victims. We are survivors. If you've been bullied, my heart goes out to you. Your emotions are valid. You are not who bullied you. You are enough. You are loved.

Since starting therapy back in 2021, I've found a love for writing letters to my inner child. During one session, my therapist suggested I write a letter to 10 year old Heather and 13 year old Heather.

That letter is as follows:

"Inner 10 year old Heather was trying to figure out why she was the target for constant bullying while also trying to get her emotions in check. Being the new kid at school was already hard for her. Add constant nagging. Constant name calling. Constant laughter from people her way as well and that left this little girl confused asf! Trying to go to adults and teachers for help yet being ignored puts more stress and anxiety on this little girl.

Inner 13 year old Heather was trying to put a stop to the constant bullying that was thrown at her and not just from kids but from family members as well. Once again, trying to regulate emotions and understand or try to figure out why it was happening left this young teenager confused. Alone. Silenced. Unworthy. Being called too skinny. Anorexic. Flat chested. Pizza face. Loner. Reaching out to adults and teachers again felt like a waste. Being told kids will be kids and you'll be fine. Get over it. THAT hurts.

To 10 year old Heather and 13 year old Heather,

"I'm sorry you had to endure such pain. Such discomfort. Such ignorance from those that are supposed to protect you. I'm sorry you had to go each day hoping you wouldn't be the target. Hoping your voice would finally be heard. I'm sorry you had to hear constant laughter from those who were supposed to be your friends. They obviously weren't your friends. I'm here to tell you tonight that everything is okay now.

Your voice matters now. You ARE heard. You ARE seen. Those words of filth thrown at you means nothing now! You ARE loved beyond measure. You ARE safe now. I got you, now! You ARE protected. Your skin glows brighter than the sun. You ARE beautiful just as is. Your beauty radiates beyond its worth.

This ride we're on together is going to be a beautiful ride. It's going to be bumpy, but we're both strong asf! We got this. I got you! I'm going nowhere, my love!"

2
CHAPTER

As I'm entering my sophomore year of high school, those thoughts of "Am I going to be bullied yet again" play in my head over and over. By this time, I'm completely traumatized. My trust for people was shattered. I've shut down with emotions. Depression starts making its appearance, but won't know what depression is till adulthood. I don't make friends as fast as everyone else. My best friend since 5th grade, she ended up moving to a new school. So, I was "alone." I did have my sister there at the school. She was a senior at this time, so that felt refreshing. During lunch, I was that "latchkey" friend. I hung out with whomever said I could. There'd be times I hung out with my sister and her friends. I did not trust anyone. I was still recovering from the previous school years.

My junior year of high school was pretty much like my sophomore year. I didn't talk much in class. I stayed quiet. Sat in the back unless our seats were assigned and I had the front row, which I hated. Haha. I'd get called on a lot. Made me so uncomfortable. Probably when my social anxiety started. Pressured to talk in class.

Lunch time I either sat by myself and walked around campus or I found some friends and just hung out with them.

Senior year is when I started to find my young voice. Rekindle some friendships from my first elementary school. This is the year I found my liking for writing. I had taken a creative writing class and fell in love with it. That class published a book and a few of my poems were selected for that year's book. I felt noticed by my peers. Accepted. It was a nice feeling. A feeling that overshadowed the hurt I was going through internally due to the deaths of my great grandmother and grandmother that had happened during Christmas break.

December 2003 was the month I lost my great grandmother Opal and my grandmother Judy weeks apart. Both from my mother's side. The two ladies that meant everything to me. They were my inspiration. They still are till this day. 20 years later. They were my motivation to finish school. Graduate on time with my class. Those two ladies were my "why" at the time. And to have them pass away months before I was to graduate high school with my class. That hurt. A hurt I didn't fully understand at the time.

December 12th, my great grandmother, Opal passed away. That day has become a blur yet I remember bits and pieces. We all knew it was coming, just not that fast. I remember being told of her passing after school. My heart ached. Granny was such a special person to me. Every chance I got to spend with her, I soaked it all in. Even going over to her trailer on weekends with my dad. I took it all in. Listened to her stories. She's my main inspiration for challenging myself and getting out of that comfort zone. She's the one soul where I get my adventurous side from. She truly lived a crazy fun filled life. I wish I had written down every adventure she conquered. Holidays were my favorite with her. She was always smiling and laughing. Wouldn't even know if she had a bad day or not. She loved her great grandchildren and it showed.

December 29th, two weeks after my great grandmother passed, five days after Christmas Eve, my hero, my grandmother, Judy passed away. I remember that Monday morning very clearly. I can even hear it right now as I'm typing this. It's a day that in my eyes tore the family to shreds. It was early morning when we got the call that grandma had passed. My sister and I were awoken to our mom screaming bloody murder, "No!" Shortly after that we hear a loud, "Jennifer" come from her. My sister and I were sharing a room at this time. We both jumped out of bed and headed out to the living room where mom was. We get mom to calm down and tell us what is going on. She tells us and right there, I knew life was not going to be the same. Not just for us, but for her.

I remember that one Christmas Eve clearly. Grandma's one wish was to have all 5 of her kids and all 8 of her grandkids home for the holidays. Her kids and grandkids were living in separate states at that time. That night, it happened. Her wish was granted. Tears were shared a lot that night. It truly was a beautiful night. Seeing ALL of us under one roof like when us grandkids were younger, was amazing. That next day, Christmas Day or following day, we all meant back over at Grandma's for family photos. Again, seeing everyone together and my family happy was just something I'll always cherish.

For me, the last time I saw my grandmother was the Saturday before she had passed. My sister and I were helping grandpa clean out Granny's trailer. Box everything up and what not. Grandpa sent us over to grandma's to get more boxes. We were told not to go in the house due to grandma being sick. She needed her rest and space. We arrive at the house, she meets us girls at the front door with a smile on her face. Tells us to come through the house to the back porch. We exchanged some words, can't recall what they exactly were, but words were exchanged. As Jennifer and I come from the back porch to the carport, our grandma opens the door and tells us to be safe and that she loves us. We do not think too much of it, we say our goodbyes and love you back. Never thinking that two days later we get the phone call that she had passed away. That Monday was a very difficult day for all of us. One I try to block out. Grandma Judy was and still is my hero in life. She's my inspiration. She was my safe place. She was truly one of a kind.

Second semester of my senior year was such a haze. I still don't know how I passed all my classes with decent grades. Of course my mother informed my teachers of what had happened during Christmas break. There'd be times some of my teachers would check in with me. I found it quite annoying yet found it refreshing saying my previous teachers had no desire of who I was. So I thought at that time.

I remember my graduation day very clearly till this day. It's a day I try to forget yet try to embrace. It was a big moment for me yet it didn't feel like it. It's a bittersweet memory for sure. I remember my grandfather Terry came over to the house hours prior, as I was getting ready, to inform me he wasn't going to make it. Which I told him I completely understand. He's still mourning the deaths of his mother and wife. Completely understand. Once he left, I remember running into my mother's arms and just balling my eyes out. My heart just crushed into a hundred pieces. The 3 main people I wanted to be at my graduation were not going to be there. It hurt so much.

That night at my graduation, it felt so surreal. Sitting on that football field looking around at everything, trying to soak it all in. Enjoy that "once in a lifetime" moment. As I'm sitting there, I get this uneasy feeling. A feeling that just didn't sit right. My main team wasn't there to cheer me on. Yeah, my parents, sister and other family were there, but THEY were not. I felt robbed.

Once the graduation came to an end and I said my "goodbyes" to my friends, I got into my dad's car and what do you know, my parents started to argue. Mom and dad were arguing about having a graduation dinner somewhere. Mom wanted it, dad said no because he had to get up for work the next morning. Remind you, I'm already hurting inside. My emotional state is high. I want to cry yet not in front of anyone. I then yell at both my parents to stop and just go home. I wanted to go home. Get away from everyone. Once we got home, tensions were high. It wasn't your hollywood perfect after graduation moment. It was just our typical night in our household. Tension. Doors were slammed. Parents were still arguing. Malerie was over at the house with us. Hanging out. Nothing too special.

When my great grandmother Opal Johnson and grandmother Judy Johnson passed away, that was the first time I experienced death. First time dealing with grief. I quickly learned that this is something we're not taught in school. Grief is different for everyone. Emotions are different for everyone. Grief is a lifelong journey as well. Doesn't stop over night. My mom was hurting just as much as I was, saying it was her grandmother and mother. She never voiced her concerns or worries with us. She kept her sadness quiet until we all went to bed. Where I got it from. Internalized emotions. I didn't know how to cope with it. I just turned 18 a month prior. That's when I found writing poems was my escape. That was my way of coping. Of grieving. Of being depressed yet not knowing it was depression til years later. When I look back at those poems, I see a hurting teenage girl. A girl who needed guidance. Needed comfort. Needed love yet it wasn't given to her.

That summer my grandfather had made the decision to sell their house and move to Kansas. Away from everyone and everything. Looking back, I don't blame him. That was his way of coping. Of healing. To say we all were very sad would be an understatement. Us grandkids grew up in that house. For me, that house held 18 years worth of memories and for them to all be gone within an instant, it hurt. My safe place was no longer my safe place. The one guy who I looked up to in life was moving hours away. Miles away. I was hurting inside. Walking through that empty house one last time was heartbreaking. Such a surreal moment for me. A moment that is so vivid till this day. 20 years later. Standing in each empty room, a ton of memories would come back. For instance, one of the back rooms was the "playroom". It had a TV with game consoles. It had a dollhouse my grandfather had made himself. All us cousins would hang out in that room a lot. If not that room, in the family room fighting over who gets to sit on the "big orange" couch watching tv. That orange couch holds so many memories, even today. Haha.

For my grandmother's twentieth anniversary, I made a post dedicated to her that I shared on my social media outlets. Every year since her passing and my granny's passing, I acknowledge them. Keep their memory alive.

"20 years without you, hard to phantom. It's crazy because we talk your name as if you're still here on Earth with us all. I miss you terribly, grandma. You were my safe place. My safe haven. My inspiration. You were who I wanted to be when I grew up. Your voice is what I miss the most. Minus your pancakes. Haha. I hope you're enjoying your time with grandpa and all yours and my other angels. Give them all hugs from me.

Here's 20 things I have achieved since your passing..

- *I graduated high school with a decent GPA.*
- *I had a few poems published in my high school creative writing book.*
- *I moved out on my own and have yet to move back home.*
- *I tried community college and Apollo College but realized that it's not for me. I'm sorry.*
- *I finally got my drivers license AND car within months apart.*
- *I've traveled to numerous states in that car. Solo and with Jen/mom.*
- *I even paid that same car off years later. Solo.*
- *I finally went skydiving like I told you I would NUMEROUS of times.*
- *I've been committed to working with kids. So many certificates and higher up recognition have been given.*

- *I was nominated and won "Teacher of the Year" for the center I worked for.*
- *I finally took that ride in a hot air balloon. It was AMAZING too!*
- *I've finally mastered some of your recipes. Yours still taste better. Haha.*
- *I FINALLY fell in love with "Heather Marie" after years of hating it. Haha.*
- *I attended a Dbacks World Series game. Not the outcome we were hoping for but the experience was phenomenal.*
- *I saw The Lion King Musical and I absolutely LOVED it. I honestly think you would have loved it as well.*
- *I've created so many paintings and with certain ones, you come to mind. My inspiration.*
- *I took your advice and continue to write. Sharing certain topics with the world. Hoping to one day write a memoir. Dedicated to you.*
- *I FINALLY went and saw the Precious Moments Chapel. You would have loved it. And yes, I still have each figurine you have given me.*
- *I finally got to witness a Dallas Cowboys home game in AT&T Stadium in Texas. Not the score I was hoping for but again, the experience was incredible.*
- *I've achieved so many small goals in these last two decades. Your voice guides me through each and every single goal.*

… I hope I have made you proud these last 20 years because your voice pushes me some days to do better. Be successful. Not letting the small stuff defeat me. I miss you. I love you."

3
CHAPTER

My grandfather Terry moved to Kansas in summer of 2004. My other great grandmother Vivian Dryden and other grandmother Kathy Rohleder both passed away in November and December of 2004. My mom's grandma and my dad's mother. Here we are yet again experiencing death and grief. This time with both parents. I knew what to expect to an extent with grief. How I can cope and how I can handle it.

Dad's way of grieving was staying quiet. Spending more time with my grandfather Victor, his dad. Or with a friend and their family. Which later brought friction towards him and my mother and me having slight jealousy against that family. He grieved very independently. Never knew he was sad. You'd think this would bring my parents closer due to having something traumatic in common. Be there for one another, like society has pictured out for couples who've just lost their family. Nope. Friction was still high in our household. Arguments still erupted in the house. Their ways of coping were completely opposite. There'd be nights I'd find myself depressed yet didn't know how to approach the situation to feel validated so I just kept to myself or I'd write. I had my sister who I'd go to often but for the most part, we all internalized our emotions.

Mine and my sister's relationship with our parents got distant to an extent. If we'd go out with friends, we really didn't have a curfew. Just had to call and check in periodically. Dad stayed back to himself as always. He worked every single day, weekends included. Jen and I ended up getting jobs. I went to a community college for half a semester. We all grew apart while living under the same roof. Not once did Jen and I get "proud of you" when we'd accomplish something special. Positive feedback was never shown amongst our parents. Why I find it very difficult to accept today as an adult who is in her late 30s. It feels uncanny to me when I'm being praised for something. I'm not one to take compliments very well. Thanks to therapy and doing the work though, I'm better than I was. When they say grief changes people, that saying does not lie. It changed my parents. My family. And till this day, I don't believe my dad fully healed before his death and my mom has yet healed 20 years later.

After graduation, I made the decision to go to Mesa Community College for Special Education. My cousin who was special needs had a huge impact on my life. The main reason I wanted to be a special needs teacher. A month in at MCC, I knew right then that this wasn't for me. Why did I want to go to college and what not you ask… to try and get away from my home life. To try and be something. I ended up going for half a semester. I dropped out. Yes, I'm a college dropout. Am I proud of it? At the time, no. Today, I'm perfectly satisfied with it. I gave it a try and realized it wasn't for me. It's not for everyone and that's what we as a society need to normalize. College is not for everyone! Let's not shame others for deciding otherwise.

I continued working at a daycare center full time instead of part time. That gave me the opportunity to start saving my money for when the time came for me to move out. It wasn't till a couple months shy of my 21st when my sister and I decided to get an apartment together. Not realizing that we'd still be roommates a decade and some years later. Haha. Just goes to show that our bond is pretty strong and the economy is a hot mess.

It was in September 2006 when we decided that we were going to move out. November I turned 21. Living away from my parents was such a release of fresh air. I was no longer surrounded by evening arguments. Negative energy. I was finally free. On my own. It was a beautiful moment. Probably one of my proudest moments. Only because not once since moving out have I had to move back home nor ask my family for any type of help. I've done it all on my own. It's such a huge achievement for me. The girl that never thought she'd be making it out on her own. The girl who never thought she'd make it thus far.

4

CHAPTER

Once I turned 21, that was when the fun started to happen. We'd get together with friends every weekend for a night or two out at the bar or club. Your typical twenty something shenanigans. Living our young lives. Experiencing "the real world." This is when social media started to get huge. Facebook is becoming for everyone, not just college students. Myspace was still popular. Everyone wants to be everyone's friend on these platforms.

Every time we'd go out, I being the kodak hoarder I am, I'd take a ton of pictures. I'd of course post some for all to see. And to me, my social media accounts are my virtual journal. A way to look back at some wonderful times. See my growth from then. Once I started posting my weekend pictures, judgment amongst family friends and family members would start circling around. I'd once again be a target for being pushed around. Yes, I'd be bullied in my adulthood for having fun with friends out at a club or bar. I'd be labeled "the weekend slut" who slept around with every guy she saw at the club. Remind you, that was not at all the person I was nor am til this day. Those rumors would make it to my mother, who did not have any social media at the time. She'd get bullied as well on the way she was parenting her girls. Crazy if you ask me. I'm a 20 something year old adult who is out having fun with her friends. An adult who does not need her mother's permission to go out on the town. My mother knew what type of person I was. She knew these people sharing this information just wanted to start drama. From the age 21 - 25 or so, I was targeted for having fun with my friends out on the town. People's assumption of me was hard to deal with. It took me back to the little girl in school who was constantly bullied. It hurt. "Family" is not supposed to hurt you yet love you. Am I not right? That's what society says anyways.

Living out on my own was also the perfect opportunity to travel. My sister and I traveled a lot. Even till this day, we're finding time to travel. We were constantly going on adventures. Concerts were our thing as well. Our way of living was causing friction amongst some family friends and family members. Harassing my mother on why she's not keeping track of her daughters. Why is she letting her girls do such things? How are her daughters able to afford all these adventures? And you know what pissed me off the most in the mix of all this? Not once did these people come to me, the source. They went directly to my mother and blindsided her with all this. People's assumptions got so bad, I stopped sharing on my social media platforms for some time. I was over the bullying. Over the drama from family members. Did it stop us from traveling and living our lives, not one bit. Did it stop us from informing our mother where we were headed? Nope. Every trip we went on, she was informed. She was never left out in the dark. She'd tell us to have fun and be safe. Still to this day, we're finding time to travel and telling her our whereabouts. Just who we've become as adults. I love it. I continue posting my pictures on my social media platforms. It's become my joy. I'm not letting others' discomfort stop me from living. Therapy again has helped me with that way of living. Put boundaries in place. Silencing the outside voices.

5

CHAPTER

When I was 22, I received a message on Myspace from an old classmate. We had Earth Science together Junior year. We sat next to one another. He was the class clown, I was the shy quiet girl who would laugh at his stupid jokes. Or I'd be the one to tell him to shut up and just listen to the teacher. Not everything needed a joke. He had a girlfriend during school so nothing ever came from me to try and make a pass at him. I didn't even find him attractive. I found him annoying. Haha.

Once he sent that message, I did not know we'd stay in one another's lives for quite some time. I never thought he'd be one reason why I am who I am today. We would continue talking for months until one night we got together for drinks out on the town. Mill Ave was our spot from the ages 21 - 23ish. We'd talk every single day and night. We'd hang out together. We'd laugh together and reminisce about our time in Earth Science. We had a good few months with one another until it wasn't good.

This relationship will define all my other relationships with men and dating throughout the years. This relationship is one that I'm not fully proud of today, but it's what I knew at the time. This relationship was not perfect at all. It emotionally, verbally and mentally drained me. Growing up in a household with parents whose relationship wasn't the greatest, it's all I knew. I didn't know what love really looked like in a relationship. All I knew was toxicity. Arguments. Manipulation. Gaslighting. Love bombing. Trauma bonding. Breadcrumbing. All I knew was red flags.

We'd argue all the time. Misunderstand one another. It'd cause friction amongst us. Not talk to one another for days or even weeks. I'm an avid journal writer & I've kept all my journals since the age of 13. This relationship takes up 3 journals. Those 3 journals are hard for me to read today. I'm getting better, but they still hold so much trauma. I'd write down some of our text conversations and just reading those today, it breaks my heart. It disgusts me. It hurts my heart for the young adult version of Heather. Had many times to get away. Get out of this relationship, yet I kept falling for his words.

I don't fully blame my dad and the way he set the bar for men in my life, but in reality, he wasn't the greatest example of how a man should treat a woman. Also, looking back, my mom didn't set a good example of self love and confidence to walk away. Our parents only do what they're learned as children themselves. I can't sit here and say what type of grandparents mine were to my mother and father, only my parents know. We learn from our parents and what was shown to us in our childhood. Take that into adulthood.

Seeing my mom stay with my dad, that told me it's okay to stay when the situation is toxic. That's exactly what I did for 4 years. I stayed in a toxic relationship hoping to feel validated and loved. To feel seen. Feel appreciated. From the age of 22 til the age of 26, I was in this ugly relationship. Many people were telling me to leave him yet I always found excuses to stay. Just like my mom would do with my dad. Find excuse after excuse to stay. Why till this day reparenting myself has been the hardest thing to do along this healing journey. Drains every ounce of emotion out of me. Angers me.

I remember the night my father passed away, I couldn't sleep, so I texted my ex letting him know what had just happened, hoping he'd show some remorse. Show some sympathy. We've already been together for 2 years. Maybe, just maybe, I'd get some type of empathy from him. Boy, was I wrong. No remorse at all. Made the situation all about himself. Which he'd often do. I was devastated yet blinded. Narcissists know EXACTLY what to say and how to act to make you fall into their trap. He did just that. Quite a lot.

2 years later, I finally said enough was enough and when I read his last words of "don't ever talk to me again," I did just that. I deleted his number that day. Took him off all my social media accounts. Moved on from him. It hurt like hell the first few months, probably the first year, only because he'd try to make his way back into my life and I wouldn't let him. And because he did it over a text and not like a mature adult face to face. In person.

The way it ended was quite ridiculous if you ask me. It was 2012's Superbowl. I just got home from a weekend in Vegas. My sister and I were given tickets to see George Strait and Martina McBride in concert that weekend. It was a great concert. Quick trip too. I just got home, turned the superbowl on. It was the year the New York Giants beat the New England Patriots. My ex was a huge Manning Brothers fan. Well, Eli was the quarterback for the Giants. I can not stand the Manning Brothers, even till this day. Not my favorite players. He knew this. We'd have silly arguments over them. It got annoying at some points. Football season with him was the worst. His opinions only mattered. Mine were invalid due to me being a girl and "not" knowing what I was talking about when in fact, I knew exactly what I was talking about. Guys just hate being outshined by women when it comes to sports. They let their ego get the best of them. He'd do that quite often.

He started to trash talk due to the Giants winning the superbowl. I was talking trash back. Thinking this conversation wasn't anything serious. Apparently, I had said the wrong thing about Eli which triggered my ex's ego and he quickly responded with "don't ever talk to me again." That right there let me know that this relationship is going nowhere as of lately and this is my calling to walk away. I responded with, "if that's what you want, I'll do as you say. So, don't talk to me anymore as well." I got no response after that. I took it upon myself to delete his number. Get him off my social media accounts. Listen to his request. Was I hurt by how he ended it, oh absolutely. Was it out of the ordinary, not at all. He was the boy who cried wolf. Similar to how my dad was growing up. When my parents got into heated arguments, my father would tell us that he's moving out. Leaving us. He never did such. Just stayed the weekend at my grandparent's house. We'd get in an argument, he'd tell me to delete his number or to never talk to him again. So, that was nothing new. My intuition that day was telling me to listen to his request for once. You've been dealing with this for far too long. It's time to get away and move on.

Months would go by and he'd try reaching out. I'd leave his texts on "read." I wasn't falling for his games any more. He'd even try to talk to me through Facebook messenger. I'd see it was from him. I'd delete the message without opening it. Years would go by and he would reach out via messenger yet again. When I saw it was from him, I stared at my phone for eternity so it felt like. I was at a work meeting on lunch break when I saw the message. All these thoughts were coming to my mind. "Why is he reaching out to me after so long. What does he want now?" It raised a lot of questions. I told myself that it's been years since then, you've moved past him. You're the bigger person now. Hear what he has to say, if anything.

So, once the meeting was over with, I took it upon myself to respond. Hear him out. Once he started talking, it's as if I was that young lady yet again. I just got an uneasy feeling from his conversation. I had mentioned to him that our relationship destroyed me. It took me a while to get over it. He did own up to his faults. Realized he hurt me and that I was a good person. He destroyed that image. He then apologized for all the stress and hurt he put me through. I accepted it. I said my side as well. I wasn't perfect in that relationship either. Said some hurtful stuff. Emotions were clearly unstable amongst us both. He then started talking and making unnecessary comments, like how I left him. I told him that I'm done talking. Said what needed to be said. Heard what he had to say. This conversation is now done and to not reach out again. It's been a couple of years since that conversation.

This relationship took so much out of me, mentally and emotionally. I wasn't ready to get back into a relationship until I was fully over what just had happened. Summer of that same year, just a few months after everything, I started working at a day program for special needs adults. I had no intentions of meeting anyone to date. My heart was still hurting and trying to heal. A couple months in, I started talking to a coworker who was the complete opposite of my last boyfriend. His mannerism was top notch. Such respect for everyone, including me. He listened when I would talk. I had no idea how to respond. I felt seen and heard for once. This was all new to me. Coming from constant arguing to calmness. It messed with my head. A month in, we made it official. Boyfriend/girlfriend official. Fall of that same year a lot was going on in my life at that time. I was in the process of moving but wasn't too sure where. Malerie's husband got the idea that all of us should move into a house together. We weren't quite sure where but thought it'd be a cool idea. I had no vehicle at that time. My boyfriend lived 50 minutes from me. Doing what I do best in hard situations, I push ppl to the side and try to focus on whatever is eating at me. I ended up pushing him away. I had mentioned to him that I needed to focus on what was happening at that moment. He respected it to an extent. We went our separate ways.

A year or so had passed. I'm living with Malerie and her family. Jen and mom were living there as well. It was literally a full house. He had reached out to me. We ended up trying to give it another chance.

I had told him everything that happened that previous year including my past relationship. He understood. A few months in, he starts getting distant. I confronted him about it. He let me know that it's hard to move forward due to what happened last time, which I completely understood. I did push him away. I did apologize for my actions. In the mix of that conversation, he tells me that his mother did call me a bitch for pushing her son to the curb. Thought that was uncalled for on her part. Very disrespectful saying she never met me. I did take full blame for my actions that night.

We were supposed to get together one weekend for his birthday. He called me that Thursday night letting me know that he needs to cancel our plans due to working all weekend. I told him it was fine. Do what needs to be done. That following Monday, I got a long text from him telling me that he lied to me about working all weekend. It wasn't true. He had a party with all his friends. They wanted to throw him a birthday party yet didn't know how to tell me without me getting hurt for not being invited. He then goes to tell me that he ended up hooking up with the girl he was talking to when we separated for that year that weekend as well. Talk about being blindsided. I was not expecting that on my lunch break. With quick judgment, I just responded with "Thank you for telling me this information, please delete my number and don't ever contact me again."

My emotional state was obviously triggered. My focus at work for the remainder of my shift was so fuzzy. I have no idea how I functioned. How I was able to teach those innocent children. All I do remember is, once I got home, I bawled my eyes out in my room alone. All these thoughts came into mind… "Was this karma from when I pushed him aside? Was this a sign to get out of the dating pool and heal my heart from my first boyfriend?" All these questions were going through my head. I've never been cheated on. Is it normal for the cheater to be up front like that? What was happening? I was in total shock. I thought at one point, he could have been "the one."

Months went by and I got a text from a random number. It was him. Trying to make conversation. Trying to apologize. I did not respond. I wanted nothing to do with him. Every few months he'd reach out. I would ignore him until one night when I finally said, let me hear him out. Let's have a solid conversation. He tells me everything from that weekend. Never apologized. Tells me that he's currently seeing the girl and that her name is mine yet she's a brunette. He's then telling me that he wants to see me. Apologize in person. I was straight forward with him. Told him to quit talking to me from that night forward. I did not need to know all that personal information about the girl he cheated on me with. After that conversation he'd still text at random moments. I'd ignore him. Kept him on "Read." Every time he'd reach out, I'd always think to myself, "why couldn't he just be up front with me and just tell me that he wanted to spend time with his friends?" I would have let him. I'm not that clingy girlfriend that he's experienced in his past relationships. If you want to go out with friends and our trust is good with one another, go live your life. Don't let me stop you. If you want to break up, tell me.

These two relationships have damaged my heart in their own ways. I damaged my own heart with each relationship. I had my faults in each relationship. I'm still healing it years later. I've been in a couple of short relationships. I've gone on countless dates yet certain situations will trigger my nervous system and then I quit the dating scene. I've been single for quite some time, only because I want to be 70% healed for the next guy. I want to heal myself. I've been on a heart sabbatical if you will. I'm done attracting what I was shown as a child. I'm done accepting less than I deserve. I'm done attracting the emotionally unstable who only want to talk due to finding me "physically attractive." I'm done seeing the color red in every relationship I experience. I want more green and less red. I deserve better!

6
CHAPTER

As I'm dealing with the breakups from my exes, I was also on the verge of ending a friendship with my best friend since elementary school. This friend only came around when it was convenient for her. When she was having issues with relationships, family and partners. She'd only come around when she wanted to go out on the town or needed to be picked up from another town.

This friend would always contact me when she was in trouble. Yell at me for not being there for her yet ignoring me when I'd share my frustrations of her not being there for me at some crucial moments of my life. She would never apologize for her actions yet expect me to apologize for mine. It started to get toxic. I wasn't having it anymore. She'd gaslight me so much towards the end of the friendship.

I remember a time very clearly when she wanted my assistance yet didn't fully understand my decision. She needed someone to come pick her up from jail due to being released. I haven't talked to her in MONTHS and had no idea she was incarcerated. It was late at night when I got the call. The city she was located in was roughly 45 mins from my house. I had to get up in a few hours for work. I had told her no. She starts screaming at me. I can't tell you what was exactly said yet I do remember her saying that I'm never there for her anymore. She figured I would be this time. I had told her I needed to get up in a few hours. I can't be there. She then hangs up on me. I didn't hear from her for a few weeks. She's then apologizing to me and wanting me to forgive her. I had told her I wasn't accepting her apology due to how she was screaming at me. I understood her emotions got the best of her yet didn't appreciate being hung up on.

After that day she contacted me, I took it upon myself to simply walk away. I was done with the one sided friendship. It wasn't mentally worth it anymore. No warnings. Nothing. I deleted her from my social media accounts. Deleted her phone number even though I knew it by heart. It was getting too much for me. As I'm doing all of this, our friendship movie started to rewind in my mind. I saw how toxic it was basically from day one yet not knowing any better due to looking for acceptance from all who came into my life at that time. I was looking for validation. Again, growing up where I didn't feel heard nor seen, any person that gave me attention, I was locked in. I was determined to be seen. Feel validated. She gave me that the very first day of school in Fifth grade.

This was the first friendship I ended. First friendship I walked away from. It was not easy by any means. This friend knew so much about my life and I knew hers. We did a lot together. She was even my prom date senior year of high school. Only because she had moved schools yet knew everyone at mine and wanted to see friends. So, me being the people pleaser I was, I took her to prom. That night was not one for the books, that's for sure. Found it very boring actually. I was never a school dance person to begin with. That was my first high school dance too. Did it for her.

I remember years had passed, last year I want to say, 2023. No contact with one another and then out of the random, I got a text from some number. I thought it was a coworker, due to how the message started. I just simply asked who this was. Boy, did that trigger her. After that convo, she went onto her social media platform and threw me under the bus without throwing me under the bus. A mutual friend had sent me the post. It was in the lines of something about not knowing your best friend. They're never there for you when you need them. Made it look as if I was the bad guy in the whole situation. She'd later make more posts about friendships. We have so many mutual friends, some of those friends would send me messages asking if those were about me. I'd answer to some yet leave others with very vague responses. It was really no one's business if we were still friends or not. She just felt the need to post about it. I wasn't.

When I was going through my first breakup, she was nowhere in sight. I'd reach out and hear nothing in return. That hurt. When my father passed away, she was nowhere in sight. All I wanted was my best friend there yet she was nowhere to be seen. Thank god for Malerie, who I met through my sister. She was there through both breakups. Dads death and so much more. She was my rock. Still is till this day. 20 something years later.

Ending this friendship let me know that it's perfectly okay to walk away from what drains you. People change. Which we both did. We've both chosen two different paths in our lives. Some of these mutual friends will still update me without me asking and she's for sure chosen her own path. I don't even recognize her at all. The only thing I can do though is wish her well and hope she finds her happiness in life.

Who knows, maybe one day we'll bump paths but until then, I'm going to continue focusing on me and my life.

As this friendship was ending, another friendship was going strong. I became friends with a coworker from one of my daycare centers. We'd go out together on the weekends. We would even go on adventures together to Disneyland. That was a lot of fun. We did a lot together.

I remember the night my dad had passed away, we were texting back and forth. Joking around. When my mother told me the news, I immediately texted my friend to tell her. I remember the exact text I sent till this day.

"My dad just died."

I'm pretty sure I confused the crap out of her. She replied with "what?" I texted her again letting her know what was going on. Told her I'd text her when I can. I remember she checked in on me days later. That was very thoughtful of her. It's who she was. Always looking out for people.

As the years went on, due to my dad's death, I started to push people away. Try to cope with his passing. She was one I started to push away. I'd only contact her when something came up that benefited me. I was doing to her what my best friend did to me. I had realized what I was doing. There was one time she confronted me about it too. It put our friendship in perspective. I did apologize to her. I saw who I was becoming with her and I did not like it. It wasn't in my character.

We did not talk for a few months or longer until it was around my 30th birthday. I wanted her to come with me to Vegas to see Britney Spears. We'd talk about it often when we were talking. I took it upon myself to reach out. Check in on her. I then asked if she wanted to take a trip to Vegas with me and Jennifer to see Britney Spears. I told her I'd pay for her ticket. For everything. It was my birthday. Something I wanted to do as did she, so I was going to make it happen. She agreed to go. We did a 24 hour stay. Left Wednesday morning. Got ready as soon as we arrived. Saw Britney Spears that night. Drove back that very next day. Thursday. She and Jennifer had to work that Friday.

That Thursday coming home was nothing out of the ordinary I don't think. Took a lil longer than expected to come home due to traffic. That Thursday was the last time I would see my friend. Months would go by and I took it upon myself to text her. Surprisingly, she responded. Asked her if everything was okay due to no contact after several months. She simply said yeah. She thought I was upset at her. Why she hadn't reached out. I told her I thought she was upset at me. Never got a full answer on what had happened. Till this day I don't know what went wrong. Once that conversation was over, I reflected on our friendship. I'm not going to sit here and say I was a perfect friend because I wasn't. I did have a lot going on but it did not give me any reason to be toxic towards her. If that's the reasoning behind why we don't talk, I'm completely okay with that. I'm owning my flaws.

This friendship was one that I thought would be life long honestly. I did not expect it to end, like how it did. Similar to how I walked away from my best friend. It's crazy how the Universe works. If later in life our paths cross, that'd be amazing. If not, that's fair as well. I wish her nothing but the best. She deserves better in life!

As I got older and smarter in some areas of my life, I realized that it's okay to walk away from friendships that aren't going anywhere anymore. It's okay if people choose to walk away from you as well. One sided friendships aren't friendships. It's okay that not everyone we meet in life will be with us forever like we want. All we can do is thank them for what was given throughout the years and hope nothing but the best for them in their life. As I do with these women. I hope they find their true happiness one day! And I would hope they wish the same for me.

Walking away from friendships is never easy, but when you have those friends who will stay by your side through every turbulence of life, it makes that transition more smooth. Having a select few people in my life since pre-teen days has been such a beautiful blessing. I ask myself every single day how I got so lucky to have these individuals in my life. What am I doing to keep them here with me? I do not take one moment with them for granted.

During my time in elementary school, I met my now life long best friend, Malerie. She and Jennifer had a class together in Jr. High. She also lived right around the corner from where we were living. Jen was outside with some of her friends and the neighborhood kids when Malerie took it upon herself to join the group. Here it is almost 28 yrs later and we're still the best of friends. She has her own little family now. I consider her 3 kids my niece and nephews. They are the absolute best and I'm not saying that to be biased at all. They truly are the best. Smart too. I love what we have created in the friendship world. You don't need the same DNA to be considered "family" as I always say!

When I was in Junior High, I took the class Home Ec. One of the classmates, Nicole, started talking with me. She was a grade ahead of me. Once we both were at the same high school, we took it upon ourselves to talk when we could. Even if it was walking down the hall to our next class. Once we both graduated and became young adults, that's when our friendship grew. Hung out more. Went out to the bar for drinks here and there. Concerts were our thing. Still are till this day. I love having her as my concert buddy. We're actually going to be attending a concert at the end of August together. Seeing a band she got me hooked on. We try to go together when this band comes into town. It only makes sense, right? Nicole has also been my go to during this time of my life. During this journey of therapy and healing. I know I can always count on her due to no judgment just listening and giving advice. She has truly been my savior during this time. I absolutely love the friendship we have. We may not see one another every single day nor month, but when we do get together, it's as if nothing changed from last time.

I consider Malerie and Nicole my two favorite women in my life. Always giving each other our flowers when due. They have helped me in more ways than they know. I am forever grateful for all these years full of friendship with them. Along with the other individuals who have been in my life for more than I imagined. You know who you are! Each and every one of them has built my character for better. Has helped me understand things. Has inspired me to do better. Every single person in my life who I consider a friend, best friend, has guided me to where I need to be at this very moment. Their guidance and advice is forever engraved in my way of living!

If you have those life long friends, go give them the biggest hug possible. Let them know what that friendship means because one day it will be gone. Let them know how they've impacted your life. Build your character. Spoke the truth without even trying to speak the truth. Give those individuals their flowers.

7

CHAPTER

September 13, 2010 around 7:00 P.M will forever be a horrible memory in my life. I remember the night like it was literally last night. It was roughly around 7 at night, I was getting ready to watch the first Monday Night Football game of that season. The Kansas City Chiefs vs The San Diego Chargers. Why I remember the teams so vaguely, a traumatic event will do that to you. You'll remember every detail as possible. It's crazy too because football was our family thing growing up. Our household was so undivided. Dad was a Green Bay Packers fan. Mom is a Chicago Bears/Kansas City Chiefs fan. My sister is a San Francisco 49ers fan. And I'm a Dallas Cowboys fan. Talk about rivalry galore. I loved it. Made for good memories.

I was relaxing on the couch when I got a call from my mother. I answer it. She's telling me that something is wrong with dad. He's slid off the couch and is now laying on the floor not responding to his name. I quickly get a pit in my stomach. I tell her to hang up from me and call 911. She does such. Calls me back and tells me he's still not breathing that she could tell. I tell her to again, hang up from me, call 911 and I'll be over there shortly. I didn't have a vehicle at the time, so I called a family member telling them what was happening. They came and picked me up. As we're driving to my parent's house, I'm talking to my mom trying to calm her down some. She's in her flight or fight mode. Emotions are through the roof. Her phone was going to die on us she kept saying. Sure enough, right when we get to the light literally right by their house, her phone dies. All I can hear is her telling me it's about to die and as it dies, I hear the "flat line." You know, the sound the machine makes when your heart stops. That's what I heard as the phone died. Sure enough, once we pulled around the corner, there's a fire truck and an ambulance. We park the car and as I'm getting out, my mom is screaming, "He's gone, Heather. He's gone." Trying to comprehend what she's saying, trying to figure out everything that is happening at that very moment, an officer approaches me asking my relations to my mother. I tell him that I'm her daughter. He then informs us that dad has passed away. They tried everything possible, but were unsuccessful. All I remember is going over to my mom and hugging her. It then dawns on me that we need to inform my sister who was at work. We then called my sister. Told her to come over to mom's house when she gets off work. That night is a night that frequently replays in my head. That phone call is one that haunts me till this day, especially when the flat line goes off. That beep haunts the crap out of me. It'll be 14 years this September and I don't think I'm fully healed. Only because it was so sudden and unexpected. And in all honesty, I'm never going to be completely healed. Accepting more than healed. If that makes sense?

That previous day, Jennifer and I were over at their house for dinner. We all were laughing and having a good time. Enjoying one another's company. Being present. We even watched the MTV Music Awards with them. Watching dad's reaction with Lady Gaga was priceless. Something I'll never forget. His death is one I'll never understand. How can one go so sudden and unexpected? We were just laughing and having a good time as a family for once. Life is so unpredictable.

Calling my grandfather that night was so hard to do. Asking if he was still awake [It was around 9pm or later] so we can stop by and share some news with him. My grandfather being the most soft spoken gentle old man he was, once he got the news that his son just passed away unexpectedly, that hurt. You could see the sadness in his eyes. You could see his soul leave his body. Not only has his wife been gone for quite some time, but now his son. His only child. He was silently hurting. I saw it. And it crushed my heart. Once we shared that news, he wasn't vocal, which was completely understandable. He was grieving his own way. Processing the news. September 13, 2010 is a night I do not wish on anyone yet someone will experience it in their own way.

Monday, September 13, 2010 is the night John Robert Rohleder passed away so suddenly and unexpectedly at the age of 49.

I remember at his Celebration of Life, everyone who knew him would come up to me and tell me how much my dad loved my sister and I. He gloated about us to his coworkers. If we did something fun as a family or father/daughter outings, he'd go to work the next day or so and gloat about his fun. He let people know how much he cared for us and loved us, yet did not really show it to us, the main people. He wouldn't even verbally tell us he loved us. So, for these "strangers" to approach me and share that with me, it left me hurting even more. It left me feeling confused. That night, I had asked Jennifer if she was told the same thing. She had told me yes and it felt weird to accept. Even today, I try to understand it yet it hurts my head so much and I give up. Only he knows his feelings.

Ever since his death, I decided I was going to live my life with courage. Do things that "scare" me. If he could go at any time, I'm pretty sure I can go at any time. Since his death, I've had all these questions that will now be unanswered. Questions I wish were asked when he was still alive yet I didn't have the courage to ask. Didn't feel the urgency to ask. His death has given me time to reflect on not just my life, but the life he was living. Trying to understand why he did what he did. Now that I'm an adult myself, some of it makes sense.

I have tried to make sense of his and my mother's relationship. Constantly arguing with one another. Constant threats of moving out. My parents were legally divorced yet stayed together under one roof til my dad's passing. If they weren't getting along, why did they stick it out? I've asked these questions as an adult yet answers are so vague. Different stories at different times. I've been trying to understand yet I don't think I fully will. Only he knows the "why" to their relationship. All I can do is break that cycle of dysfunctional relationships.

For anyone who has lost a family member either unexpectedly or expected, know that your emotions are completely valid. No matter your relationship with this family member, your emotions and memories are valid. We will experience death in different ways, and grieve differently as well. Embrace those memories that will come forward. Sit with the negative ones, they are just as valid as those good memories.

8

CHAPTER

Skydiving was something I've wanted to do since high school. My 25th birthday was coming up, a couple months after my dad's passing. I knew I had to do such. Growing up my great-grandmother, Opal, was such an adventurous lady. She skydived in her later years. In her 70s I believe. I knew I wanted to do such a thing as well in my life. I figured why not do it for my 25th. That birthday is a milestone for all. Why not go big and accomplish something even bigger for myself.

Everything was set in stone. Family was going to help me fulfill this dream of mine. All this planning was already set before my father's passing. As the time got closer, we were still dealing with dad's belongings and what not. Had to sell his vehicle. Donate his belongings. Cancel his name with all his bills. The small things people don't mention when death happens.

My mother gave my sister and I our share from what she got from selling dad's truck. When the week of my birthday was approaching, I had contacted this family member to make sure it was still okay for them to help me with this adventure. I did not hear from this individual yet I got a call from my mother asking me what was going on and why is this individual yelling at her over the phone. I had told her that I asked this individual if they could help me and they agreed. All I was doing was checking in to see if they were still able to help. I had also told my mother that this agreement happened before dad's passing. So, for them to call her and not me was semi mind-boggling. Remind you though, from previous years of people contacting my mother about us, they don't go to the source. They go to others about the source. Just who they are as individuals. Something I still don't understand today. My mother, sounding confused over the phone, had told me this family member was on their way to her house and that we needed to be there as well.

Jennifer and I arrived at my mother's house. Trying to figure out what was going on. Why was this individual acting the way they were? They arrived pounding on the door and started screaming and yelling at us. Not giving us time to speak our truth. When we did start talking, we would get cut off. This person was making the situation about themselves. This individual was verbally attacking us for no apparent reason. I was once again called a "slut." I was called a bitch as well. My mother was called an "unfit" mother due to her girls going out every weekend and one "sleeping around with every guy she sees." They're calling Jennifer a "bad" big sister for letting her younger sister do what she does out on the town. This person was just verbally attacking us left and right. Their emotional state was obviously triggered. It had NOTHING to do with my birthday weekend at all. This person targeted us at our lowest points in life. My mom just lost her ex husband. The father to her girls. Her friend since high school. She's still grieving. My sister and I are still grieving. Did this family member care, not at all. And I stand on that till this day.

That night opened my eyes of who this individual was and my relationship with them would soon fade. We at one point had a close relationship. They were there when my parents weren't. Or when my father wasn't. They'd help out every way they could growing up. Some of it was asked, some was voluntarily, while some was to make others look "unfit". Make it look as if they're the "perfect" person. Looking back, it was all about being in control. Manipulators LOVE being in control. Gaslighting others to make them believe they're in the wrong when it's the manipulator who is clearly in the wrong.

That night was yet another trigger of all those times I was bullied in school and bullied for living my life. It was not making any sense to me. Why am I the target of getting bullied? Getting belittled? The more I sat on it, the more it made sense. I was an easy target. I was the quiet one. The most vulnerable one. And the bullies knew it. I didn't know how to emotionally handle situations. My freeze response would be activated. To say I'm still healing from all the abuse that has been thrown my way [verbally, mentally, and emotionally] would be an understatement. So much self love and self confidence was taken from me. My voice was taken away from such a young age. Wasn't fair.

I remember that Saturday morning of the skydiving trip, the company had called me letting me know they had to cancel due to high winds that day. I quickly got upset and started to blame this family member for putting the bad energy in the air yet later in the day thanking the Universe for canceling due to not having to deal with certain people. That night I told myself that we're going out and we're going to have a good time. I'm not going to let this unnecessary event ruin my birthday. So, I texted a few friends and we headed off to the bar to have a great time.

Shortly before dad passed away, my parent's just signed their lease for the apartment they were staying in. My mom was financially struggling. There was another family member who took it upon themselves to move in with my mother during again, her most vulnerable time of life. Looking back now, these individuals like to target the vulnerable and make the situation about them. Not giving 1% about the other person. I'll stand on that till the end of time. This member of the family was going through their own issues and needed a place to stay. My mother being the gentle soul she is, the people pleasing human, she said yes. Thinking they'd get their life together and help out with finances. Boy was she wrong. This person took full advantage of her and I'm sure still till this day sees no fault in their actions from that time period.

I remember Jennifer and I had to help mom financially on top of our finances. It was not easy by any means. It was chaotic and stressful. Her living situation with this person brought her so much stress. Brought us stress as well. So much depression. She felt alone. Her family wanted nothing to do with this situation. We financially made it work for that year. Once that year approached us, we came to the conclusion that she could move in with us girls. That individual got upset at us for not thinking about them. I'm sorry but you're a grown adult who is making these decisions. You now have to pay for your consequences. My sister and I were raised where handouts weren't the answer. You had to work for what you wanted. What you needed. That's one life lesson I'm forever grateful for with my father.

Once my mother moved in with us, my life at that moment changed. It got quiet. I wasn't the adventurous person I was when I moved away from home. It's as if I was living back at home. I shut down. My relationship with Jen faded. Mine and my mother's relationship grew further apart. We'd get into some arguments. Name calling would happen on her part. It was just a tough patch of my life at the moment. It caused so much stress on me. Caused so much anxiety. But at the same time, my mother had nowhere to go. Her family wasn't much help. Would downgrade her on certain occasions. They even belittled my sister and I for helping our mother. So, we took it upon ourselves to help her get her life together.

Years later she would eventually move to Missouri. Her choice. She brought it to our attention one night. Jennifer and I were all for it. She needed this. She needed to find herself again. We encouraged her to take the leap and go with her gut. It's now been roughly 6 years or so. Our relationship is still not great but we're working on it.

Thanks to my therapist. I do tell my mother that I'm proud of her for taking that leap. She needed it. Grant it, I was never praised for doing good in my life, but I'm not those people. I'm breaking cycles. So, every chance I get to let my mother know I'm proud of her, I tell her. Some days it's really hard, not going to lie, but I do it for me. It's part of my healing process. I'm still working on accepting the "I'm so proud of you" statement as well. It's different, that's for sure. I keep telling myself if I want to fully heal, this is part of healing. Accepting the uncomfortable.

Reparenting myself these past couple of years has not been easy by any means but I'm doing it. I'm doing it for little Heather. She deserves it the most. I'm doing it for future Heather. She needs that happiness again, which she will get! There's been nights of crying myself to sleep. There's been days of feeling frustrated at my mother for not being "there" for me. I've had moments of wanting to give up on myself due to not being "healed" already. I then give myself a little pep talk of not giving up. I've come so far in my healing journey. Therapy has been a great help as well. Some days are harder than others but in the long run, everything will be okay. I'm beyond proud of myself for doing such.

9
CHAPTER

Six years after dad's passing (2016), my grandfather, Victor, passed away. That weekend is one I'll forever remember as well. As per say, grief and trauma will do that to one's memory. This weekend was one that defined my strength. Strength I did not know existed in me.

He's been in the ICU for roughly a couple of weeks at this moment. It was a Sunday afternoon, Jennifer, mom and myself went and visited with him not realizing that would be the last time we'd ever see him again. I for one hate hospitals. One of my last not so happy memories of hospitals was with my grandmother Kathy (his wife). Ever since that moment, I have found a slight dislike for them. So walking into that hospital room seeing my grandfather all covered up with blankets and towels on his face and whole body was so unreal. He was unrecognizable. Felt like I was trapped in a nightmare. The nurse did inform us that he wasn't very responsive with them that day, maybe we can get him to respond to our cues. My mother and sister were in shock. They didn't know how to react nor how to approach the situation to get him to respond. Which was perfectly okay. Me being me, I took it upon myself to do such. I was in shock as well, but

I wasn't going to dwell on the situation. I wanted my grandfather to be okay. I wasn't ready for him to go. Not like this.

I remember walking up to his bed, grabbing his very cold and fragile hand and asking if he could hear me. If so, grab my hand. As I'm slowly sitting down in the chair beside his hospital bed, I felt him grab my fingers tightly. Like a little kid holding their parents' hand to cross the street. Safety hold. My heart dropped to my toes and I felt this heavy feeling on my chest. I got this lump in my throat as well. As I'm typing this sentence, I can get his touch on my fingers. Sends chills through my body each time. Makes my eyes water each time as well. It'll be 8 years this October since his passing and I can still feel his touch on my hand. Something I'll forever cherish. I also asked him if he could hear me to open his eyes very slowly. He opened his eyes very faintly. Squinted his eyes due to the brightness of the light and having that rag on his face for as long as he did. That broke my heart the most yet put my mind at ease knowing he is coherent. As I'm nervously removing the cloth from his face, I get a pit in my stomach. That was not the grandfather I knew. He looked defeated. We spent a little more time with him. Holding his very cold and fragile hand. Telling him we love him and if he's ready to go and be with his family, we'll be okay with it. Once I got home, my heart and mind was not right. I wasn't ready for my grandfather to go yet I knew he was going to pass very soon.

After my dad passed away, us girls would go over to his house and spend time with him. He didn't have much family left. We'd take him grocery shopping every Sunday. We'd go over to his house every Thanksgiving and Christmas Day. We would take care of him. Visit with him. Spend as much time as we can with him. Listen to his stories of his war days. He enjoyed sharing his stories. I loved listening to them. Wish I had written them down though. I've forgotten some. He even shared some stories about my dad from when he was younger.

That following Monday morning, the VA hospital had called us girls yet left a message with our mother saying that he had passed away in his sleep. Same day of the week his son had passed six years prior. When I woke I saw the number but didn't recognize it. Something inside of me knew it was the hospital yet part of me did not want to believe it. I went ahead and went into work. I had informed my bosses of what was going on so if they receive a call from either my sister or mother, that is why. I wasn't even at work for a couple of hours when one of my bosses came into my classroom. Once I saw her, I knew EXACTLY why she was there. All she had to do was look at me. No words exchanged. I just remember breaking down in her arms in front of my students and co-teacher. That day was a hard day. Dealing with grief for yet another time. I think about that day often. Breaking down in my boss's arms. Wondering if she randomly thinks of that day as well.

That day in the hospital was the first for me. Something I did not see in my deck of life cards. Something I thought I'd never experience. Today, I'm grateful I was there in that hospital room that day. I'm grateful for the grab he gave me after the nurses said he wasn't responsive that morning. Grant it, that may have been the last memory with him and one that unfortunately replays in my head, but it's one that I'm grateful for. Therapy has taught me to find gratitude in grief. And that's what I did with this passing. Found gratitude in it. It showed me just how strong I truly am. If I can experience something this tragic, I can handle whatever else life has to offer me from that day forward. It showed me resilience.

The day of his funeral was just as hard. It was an open casket. Something I've never experienced. Everyone that had passed on before him was cremated. This was something totally new and out of my comfort zone. He looked so peaceful yet did not look like the grandpa I knew. It was hard. I did not like who I saw. I was also informed by one of his family members that I'd be reading his obituary outloud in front of everyone. Talk about panic attacks without knowing what a panic attack was. Again, something I've never experienced in my life. Reading his obituary in front of everyone was extremely hard to do. Standing by that podium, I was shaking tremendously as I was reading his obituary. Bawling my eyes out as well. I don't even know if anyone could comprehend what was being said. I do recall Jennifer walking up on stage and hugging me. Holding me as I continued to read. Everything else from that day has become a blur. Trauma response. Our brain tends to "erase" certain events in our life that feel too heavy.

With him being a veteran, he chose to have the proper send off with "Taps" being played and the presentation of the flag, which was given to Jennifer due to my father being the only child and already deceased. She's the oldest granddaughter, so everything that had to deal with my grandfather, she was the go to person. Sitting next to her as the soldier is folding the flag was something I'll never forget. I can't share her feelings or emotions because I don't know what she was going through, but for me to witness such, that was hard on the sister heart. Something I did not see us experiencing in life together at the age we were. Dad was "supposed" to get the flag.

Cleaning out his trailer after his death was such a headache. Only because he had a few family members alive and they didn't want much of his belongings. My grandmother's family was unreachable, so it was just up to us girls on deciding what happens to their belongings. My grandfather still had a few months left on his lot lease, so, my sister and I had to pay that fee on top of our own personal monthly fees. It took a toll on us yet again. Financial anxiety would be high yet not fully knowing what financial anxiety was at the time. Once that trailer was empty, I think that's when it hit me. I no longer had a reason to go to that trailer. A trailer that held 30 years of memories. That trailer was the last of my dad and his story. A story of the Rohleder clan as I like to call them. When we were in the process of cleaning it out, being the journal writer I am, I remember that entry very clearly…

"The number 125 to you may be just three numbers, but to me, those numbers hold 30 years of my life. 30 years worth of love, life, laughter, and sorrow. 30 years worth of unforgettable moments that are now forever memories. Closing

that door for the last time will be one of the hardest things I'll have to do in life thus far. Knowing I won't be able to go back whenever will be the toughest. Thank you Grandpa Rohleder for some of the best days of my life."

Once my grandfather, Victor Rohleder, had passed, I would post simple memories on my facebook. Like that journal entry for example. Every time we were out and I saw an elderly man wearing their veteran's hat (just like my grandfather would wear), I'd go and thank them for their service. I took it as a sign from my late grandfather. Letting me know he's there with me. I'm a very spiritual person. I believe that we do come back and visit our loved ones in different forms. Whether it be in white feathers, butterflies, random pennies on the ground, songs, vehicles, random strangers and other forms, I believe they are there with us.

When I'd post on my social media these special moments, so I thought they were special, I'd always get that one negative comment from a certain individual. I would not interact back for one, it being public for all to see and two, for them wanting to start drama. Making it about them yet again. I'd just ignore the comments. There was a time I stopped sharing my personal thoughts and memories on my social media accounts due to the negative feedback I'd get from this person. Always making it about them and belittling me of why I never recognized my other grandfather during certain times. Yes, I let them win at that moment. Once I realized that, I told myself to keep embracing the memories I have with my late grandfather. Their actions define them, not me. They don't know the full truth behind my relationship with my grandfather, Terry. I'd also find out later on, it brought out jealousy amongst other members of my family when I'd share my thoughts, memories and what not about my grandfather Victor. Crazy how something so special to one can have such a huge negative impact on another.

10

CHAPTER

From everything that was happening in my life, so much was weighing on my heart. So much was weighing on my shoulders. I felt it. It felt like a huge 50 lb backpack full of bricks. It was all finally crashing on me. Even years after the fact. Everything was crashing down on me. At the time, I didn't know it was anxiety. That word was non-existent in my vocabulary. I had no clue what it even was while all these traumatic events were taking place.

I'd experience random very faint chest pains. Didn't think much of it saying they'd go away minutes later. I'd have moments where my mind would be racing non stop. The "what ifs". Sleep was even becoming non-existent. Insomnia became my nightly bestie. Nothing was calming it down. I'd have moments where my body would be frozen. I was unable to move. People would catch me just staring off into space. Later to find out, I was dissociating. Trauma response. My body was holding every emotion possible until a simple task would come around and then I'd start feeling anxious. Start sweating uncontrollably. My vision would get blurry. Eyes would also burn. I'd shake as if I was nervous yet nothing was happening to get nervous over. I was constantly feeling stressed. Trying to control the uncontrolled. You name it, I was experiencing it.

I had just transferred to a new daycare center where I'd train to be part of the management team and not in the classroom. It was going so good until a couple months in, a tragic event happened where it put a toll on my stress level. One I never experienced while in this field. And I've been in this field for 20 years now. 14 years at the time. This traumatic event caused new management to come in and take charge a few months later. This event taught me so much about my abilities as a Team Lead. My strengths and my weaknesses. I realized once things started to get tough, I'd quit. One of my coworkers at the time saw it as well. She'd encourage me to do better. Get my confidence strong. As the months went on into the following year, I'd start getting these non stop chest pains. My body would tense up. I'd get these heavy headaches, migraines if you will. I'd play it off like it was nothing. Once the chest pains didn't go away for two weeks straight, I knew something was wrong. With the way my dad passed away, I knew I needed to go get checked. Even my boss at the time told me to go get checked. Could be serious.

I remember I made an appointment in August of 2017. I had told the doctor everything that was going on. We did an EKG. Ran different tests, tests I can't recall today. Come to find out, I was experiencing anxiety and panic attacks. When my body would go numb. Chest pains. Migraines. Anxious feeling. Those were all signs of anxiety and panic attacks. When the doctor shared the results with me and told me I have Generalized Anxiety Disorder or GAD, I was left confused. I had never heard of the words anxiety or panic attacks. Anxiety was never spoken around me nor to me. When I say the car ride home was such a blur today, I'm not lying. It's like my rewind button of life was pressed. Everything was coming back to me. Certain events and actions were coming back to me. It was all making sense.

August 2017 changed my life. It may sound so cliche, but it has. It puts my previous situations into perspective. It's allowed me to understand life today and why my body reacts the way it does. Of course there's days and moments where my anxiety takes over, but after all these years and after all the research I've done and continue doing, I know how to regulate my nervous system. How to calm the nerves. The way I describe anxiety to those who don't experience it is this, it's like that lingering hair you can't find on your shirt, you know it's there but you can't find it. It's also like a hamster who goes full speed on their hamster wheel and has trouble stopping. That's what it feels like. Your mind and body are stuck on flight or fight constantly. Or if you've seen the Pixar movie, Inside Out 2. The way they portrayed Anxiety was top notch. That's what I've been dealing with.

Once I found everything out, I told myself that I wasn't going to let something like this control me. I'm going to continue living my life doing what I need to in order to survive and have fun. I also told myself to share certain situations, to be the voice for the shaken. For those who don't know of such. Educate others so they are aware of those around them. I told myself to make it a mission to normalize mental health issues. Don't be scared to share my story. Let the vulnerability side show. Let others know it's okay. Being vulnerable is not a scary thing. It's a beautiful thing.

August 2017 has taken me down so many different roads, roads I would have never imagined I'd travel down. This journey is not for the weak, that's for sure. If you are traveling down this road, I'm here to let you know, you are not alone. You are enough. Your voice matters. You are worthy. You are not your anxiety. You are not your diagnosis.

If you are someone who experiences anxiety, what do you do to calm your nervous system? Do you know your triggers that can activate anxiety? Do you practice mindfulness? Find gratitude in your days? Do you speak affirmations into existence? What are some things in your toolbox to calm those nerves?

If you're someone who knows someone with anxiety and wants to educate yourself, start here, be patient with that individual! Let them come to you when their anxiety is "flaring" up. Don't pressure them to talk. Advise them to take deep breaths. Let them know you're not going anywhere. Give them positive reassurance. Listen to them without judgment. If you've made plans and they cancel the day of, don't get angry at them. Their body is more than likely on overdrive. They need rest.

When my anxiety is trying to come through, I repeat this affirmation as many times as needed until I feel at ease. "I am safe!" When I'm experiencing an attack, I like to repeat this affirmation as many times as needed, "you are not your anxiety" as I'm doing deep breathing techniques. I also find gratitude as a helpful tool. Being an avid journal writer, each morning I write 3 things I'm grateful for, the first one ALWAYS being "I'm grateful for the air in my lungs at this given moment" and each night I write 5 things I'm grateful for, that being the first one as well. When my anxiety is high, I reframe my negative thoughts and find that day's silverlining. Grounding is another technique I find helps.

Anxiety does not define me nor you! We define who we are. Who we want to be. Some lingering "mental illness" will not! I believe in you. I am here for you.

11

CHAPTER

Growing up, dad would let us drive his truck in a big empty parking lot. Thought it was the coolest most "grown up" thing to do as a kid. He'd also let us drive his car around the block, unsupervised. We'd even sneak away and go on the public roads. Test the limits. Like any other teenager. Not one ounce of nervousness to be shown. No care in my unsupervised teenage life.

Once I got into high school, as a sophomore, I took Drivers Ed. My high school at the time had a driving range. I do recall, every time it was my turn to take the wheel, I'd get extremely nervous. I'd tense up. Have racing thoughts of hitting the other car or another car hitting me. My palms would get all sweaty and shake. I'd feel my face get all flesh and hot. All signs of anxiety. I remember a time where we had to do the 3 point turn and I couldn't get it right. Everyone else got it right on the first try except me. There were others in the car as well. I remember them all talking at once to turn the wheel this way and my teacher who was on the car radio telling me to go that way. I was intensely overwhelmed to say the least. My body completely shut down and I completely froze. The passenger saw such and told me to drop my shoulders, unclench the steering wheel and to take a deep long breath. Everything will be alright, they reminded me. They let me know that it was fine to take my time parking. Ignore the outside noise and just focus on what's in front of me. I still find myself repeating that till this day. I ended up parking the car. I do recall once we got back to the class, everyone was making small talk about me very quietly with one another. I felt it in my body. I wanted to go home and hibernate. Walking to my next class felt like the longest walk that day.

While taking Drivers Ed, I thought why not try for my permit. I was of age. My confidence was at its peak. Every time I went for my permit, I'd flunk the test. Until that one day after multiple tries, and when I say multiple tries, I mean it. I finally got my permit. I felt proud of myself. No one in my family verbally said such. They'd for the most part internalize it or respond with "it's about time." Once it expired, I would go and try for my drivers license. Again, not passing. Test anxiety was real. Not realizing it at the time, but I'd always freeze up during tests. Even in school, I'd freeze up and forget everything I knew. Studying for the test was pointless even though I'd still do such. The night before AND the morning of. I was eventually experiencing test anxiety.

I had given up on trying to get my license. Gave up on myself. Confidence was no longer there. My parents' help and encouragement was invalid. There would be times I'd drive my friend's car or sister's car without the proper identification. I of course would be careful. Drive the speed limit. Watch for law enforcement. All that proper stuff. There'd be times my anxiety would take over, not knowing at the time what it was. Once I would get home, I'd feel such a relief in my body. Even with passengers, I'd get nervous. Still do. Hands would be sweaty. Mind would be racing. Vision would get blurry. It was all my anxiety. But again, I had no idea what anxiety was until years later.

Up until the age of 31, I'd bum rides from family members and friends to get to and from work. Just the thought of getting behind the wheel scared me. Which was weird due to driving all those other times. I would even feel anxious as the passenger. Thinking we'd crash or someone would crash into us. I wouldn't say anything to the driver. I'd internalize it, like everything else.

I remember I was waiting for my ride to come pick me up from work one day and as I'm sitting there, I started to get annoyed at myself. I started to yell at myself for relying on people. Feeling guilty as well. Here they are taking time out of their day to cater to me, much appreciated to say the least. I was doing what my mother would do. Made me realize I did not want to rely on people for as long as time allowed. I needed to get my license. Start depending on me. That night when I got home, I wrote in my journal. Yelling at myself. Talking down to myself. Reminding myself I'm a grown adult who should not be relying on others. Break that cycle. Don't be like others in the family. That day was my wake up call.

March 17, 2017 was the day I finally got my driver's license. At the age of 31. I finally shut up the negative voices in my head. Finally stopped self-sabotaging myself and proved to not just me but to everyone else who was doubting me and comparing me to others, that I am capable of breaking those cycles and overcoming those "fears." Two months later, I bought my very first car. A red Chevy Cruze. That was exciting yet nerve wrecking. Saying I had no idea how the process went about. Thank god I had Jennifer and Malerie with me. Those girls are my everything, even till this day, they are my go-to people. I absolutely love you Jennifer and Malerie!

A month later, in June, I drove my car to Iowa. I was nervous to take this trip. It would be my first time driving a very long distance. Grant it, I had my sister and mother with me, but it was still nerve wracking. There would be a few moments of my driving anxiety coming through, especially on the highways. That trip was just the beginning of many adventures with my car, Turbo, as I like to call it.

That next year, my sister and I took a trip to Missouri, with not just her car but with a moving truck. Talk about every negative emotion trying to creep in my head. My mother had just moved to Missouri a few months prior. We were taking her belongings to her. I drove the majority of the way in the moving truck, only because I wanted to test my limits. Test my anxiety. Once I was told I had anxiety, I told myself from that day forward I wasn't going to let it control me. I was going to do anything and everything to not let it affect me.

There were quite a few moments where my anxiety was high. One being in the mountains and driving along those roads. I'd grip the steering wheel so tight that it'd leave my palms all red. I even got blisters. That's how bad I was gripping the steering wheel. Other times would be on the state highways during construction. First time driving a big vehicle in construction. Talk about a great time. Haha. That trip to Missouri helped me realize what exactly driving anxiety was. Helped me recognize my anxious moments. It put a lot of situations into perspective. Once I got back home to Arizona, I did some research on ways to calm the nerves while driving.

Till this day, I'll experience moments of driving anxiety but I now know how to handle those difficult situations. For instance, I have a soft steering wheel cover. When I feel the anxiety, I'll start rubbing the steering wheel. Sensory stimulates the nervous system. I'll also call out whatever is in front of me. Similar to the game "I Spy." Distract the mind. I also keep peppermints in my car. People think it's hilarious. Always joking about my breath but in reality, it's to help stimulate and distract the mind of taste. When I'm really anxious, I have to turn the radio down, not up. Loud noises in tiny areas overwhelm my nervous system. Different I know. My therapist was shocked too when I told her about the music.

I've tested my driving anxiety so much. Again, I'm not going to let it affect my life. I'm in control of my life, not this disorder. I've traveled to many places just so I could test my anxiety. I drove to Colorado by myself. I've traveled to different cities here in Arizona by myself. The most recent trip I did was to San Francisco in 2024. That trip challenged my anxiety to a tee. It's what I wanted though. What I needed for myself. I do these trips to challenge the nerves. Test my limits. It's helped me in so many ways, surprisingly. I encourage those of you who do have driving anxiety or anxiety in general to test yourself. You will learn so much about your triggers and what works to calm those triggers. You will learn more about your nervous system. Driving anxiety is a real thing and I want to let you know, you too can overcome such. I've enclosed some tips and affirmations to help calm your nerves.

If you are a writer, keep a journal in your car and write down your experiences. When and where your anxiety peaks the most. What specific situation triggered it. I do such and it's helped me tremendously.

Keep peppermint gum or mints in your car. It helps to stimulate the nerves. Focus on the taste of it. Smell of it. How does it taste? Is the smell strong?

Texture is another tool to use in stressful situations. For me, I have a soft steering wheel cover I'll rub when I start to feel anxious. I also keep a hair tie on my wrist to fidget with. How does the steering wheel cover feel on your hands? Is the texture soft? Bumpy? Hard?

I've even learned from therapy to use positive affirmations in certain situations. For my driving anxiety, I like to use these affirmations..

I trust my driving skills and ability to handle any situation.
Challenges on the road are opportunities for me to grow as a driver.
The steering wheel feels comfortable in my hands, extension of my focus.
I trust my instincts and react with confidence behind the wheel.
I flow smoothly with the traffic, maintaining a safe distance.
Even in traffic, I can enjoy the ride and appreciate the scenery.
I trust my judgment and feel empowered on the highway.
I arrive at my destination safely and securely, even after dark.

Driving anxiety can be nerve-wracking for some, I know. If you're one who battles, know you are not alone. You're stronger than these triggers. You're wiser than those "fears." You too can overcome such.

12

CHAPTER

In October 2018, I came to the decision on finding a weekend job. A second job if you will. Finances were going up along with my financial anxiety. Financial stress every month was real. My anxiety was going through the roof. Living paycheck to paycheck was something I told myself I did not want to do. I saw it growing up with my parents. Asking for financial help was not something I wanted to do as well. Saw it growing up. Was not who I wanted to be. Not because it was shown as a sign of weakness, when in reality, it's perfectly okay to ask for help, but because I was shown and taught to work for what we needed and wanted. Handouts weren't acceptable. Till this day, I'm grateful we were shown the value of a penny as I'd like to say. It's built my character. It's taught me so much about the world. It has humbled me so much. Being financially stable has guided me into the right direction of financial freedom.

After posting on facebook of jobs hiring for part time and weekends, I had a friend/old coworker of mine, Gina, reach out. She was working with Special Need adults in independent living. I had asked her if this job was hiring. She gave me her boss's information. I reached out to her boss the next day and that following week I had an interview and was hired days later.

When I started this job, I was working 7 days. No days off. Everyone was telling me to be careful and watch my mental health. I knew what I was doing at the time. Letting them know that this job is actually my down time from my main job puts them at ease. My finances got better. Having cushion money as I like to call it has been a blessing. It's allowed me to do so much traveling. Attend concerts. Live my life full of adventure. How I want it to be.

Three years in, my main job started to get stressful. Started to become beyond toxic. First job that I had going this way. Was trying to comprehend everything. Once again, control the uncontrolled. Anxiety's favorite thing to do to me. Stress levels were high. My body was screaming at me to take a rest day. This job was becoming stressful with a client. I had asked my boss if I could drop Saturdays and keep Sundays. She agreed to the situation. Boy, with my main job, having that one day off was such a help. I'm very clear that it's a "I told you so" situation, but again, this was something that I needed to do for me. Figure out on my own.

Here I am years later still working both jobs. I did not expect it to last this long. I was just looking for a temporary weekend job to help with finances. Which is still going great. Was able to pay off the little debt I had. Pay off my car. It's not the glamorous life as some see it, but again, this was something I needed to do in order to be okay. This is my life and I've made the best of it.

Having my friend here with me at first on the weekends made the days seem so calming. Wasn't stressful like a job would be. She later had to leave due to family situations. I still thank her for reaching out and giving me our boss's information. If it wasn't for me posting on facebook asking for weekend job ideas and her commenting on the post, I don't know where I'd be financially. Probably stressing out, like I tend to do over situations that will all be okay within hours or days. Good ole anxiety and it's never ending tactics.

Everything was going so well with both jobs, even after getting to have Saturdays off until it wasn't anymore. I started to slip back into this dark hole. The dark hole of when I was in high school. The depression started to creep back in. My confidence was disappearing. My self love was fading. Rejection from trying to find a better week day job was very high. Nobody would hire me due to lack of experience or high pay. I had no desire to do anything but sleep on my only day off. I'd constantly fake it to make it during the weeks. Even on Sundays, I'd fake a smile. Keep it professional. My anxiety was getting bad. I was not liking who I was becoming at all. I've been known to be such a positive person yet I had no light left in me. I was drowning in this dark hole. I wanted out. I needed to get out. I was done living in survival mode. I was done always being in fight or flight mode. I was done letting past traumas affect some of my days. I was just done with it all.

One Sunday while talking about current life situations, Gina would share that she was going to therapy. The more she shared her experiences and progress, the more it sounded like something I wanted to do. I needed to do. I'd always crack a joke growing up that when I'm an adult, I'd be sitting on some random person's couch sharing my problems. That kept replaying in my head over and over. Do I really need therapy or am I exaggerating like anxiety would do periodically? The more I sat on the idea, the more I realized, I do in fact could use therapy in my life. Help guide me to a better version of myself. We can't go back to what once was. We can only go forward and create better. I wanted better. I needed better.

13

CHAPTER

In October of 2019, Gina gave me the information of the therapy office she was attending. I then filled out the paperwork to start my therapy voyage. To see a therapist. It felt embarrassing at first. Thank goodness for Gina to calm my nerves and let me know that it's perfectly okay to see a therapist. They're here to help us not judge us. I've been judged my whole life til then. That was refreshing to hear at the moment. Once my paperwork was filled out, I got a call a few weeks later from the office assigning me to a therapist.

Sharing my life story thus far with this therapist was overwhelming to say the least. I felt nervous to share. Nervous of being judged. My body was shaking and I was sweating during this first session. It was via Zoom, virtual, and with my lack of self confidence and not liking who I see stare back at me in the mirror, this was very intimidating. Yes, I'd share bits and pieces via social media but nothing like I did at my very first full session. I would keep my sharing very vague on social media. Hearing it come out word for word, event for event was eye opening. I did feel as if I was oversharing. I'm noticing that what had happened to me thus far was heartbreaking. Keeping the peace growing up for others' satisfaction was no longer in my way of living. Enduring all that I did was no longer how I wanted to treat myself. I knew once I started therapy, a lot of wounds were going to be opened. I knew my shadow would want to come out and play as well. I was ready for it. I was ready to heal. To heal my voice. To heal the little girl inside of me. To heal what was taken from her.

I was with that therapist for a little over a year until she was switching companies. I was then assigned to another therapist, who still till this day, I loved having. She put everything into perspective. Got me to write to that inner child. She encouraged me to do shadow work when journaling. She's the one who got me to journal more than I was already doing. And then report back to her on our next session. That was something I wasn't ready for. My journal entries are just that, mine. So for me to read them outloud, that took a lot of courage on my part. I did tell her to test me and my limits. Challenge me. I'm ready to grow, not stay little. Reading those entries were so hard at first but as the sessions went on, I felt okay reading aloud to her. My voice would tremble during certain readings. That's when I learned more about vulnerability and how it can be a good thing as well as being a scary thing. Roughly six months with her, she informs me that she will no longer be my therapist. That hurt. I was healing wounds thanks to her and her dedication to help me. To push me to work harder. She was a good therapist. Experienced therapist. Which I liked.

I was later given a therapist that was hard to connect with. Maybe because I was playing the compare game with my previous one. This therapist didn't push me as hard. I'd leave my sessions not feeling like I got anything accomplished. This therapist would just focus on the fact that I journal every night. Would give me prompts to use. Wasn't really healing with those. There was one point where I had asked if we were going to get into the healing aspects or just talk like two best friends. I think it upsetted her due to our next session, we started to heal certain wounds. She had me do EMDR for a few months. That technique was brutal. Brought back certain memories of my life that I didn't know needed full on healing. I thought they were already healed. If you don't know EMDR stands for Eye Movement Desensitization and Reprocessing therapy. It's a technique to help with traumatic events. It helped me understand certain situations that took place in my life growing up even though it was hard to relive again.

After those few months were over, she went back to being my friend. Not much was getting accomplished. I took it upon myself to do a self discharge. I was already reading books, doing workbooks from an author I've been following while starting this journey. I decided I wanted to self heal. I already had some tools in my toolkit. I already knew what to do when things started to get bad again. That lasted for a good couple of months until I started falling back into that dark hole. Back into bad habits. I decided to reach out to another friend who was also going to therapy. She passed down the info and here we are, on therapist number four. I like her. She's an experienced lady. What I wanted. Not a young therapist. Someone with life experiences under their belt. It's been the best decision thus far. So much has changed in this short period.

Therapy has taught me about boundaries and how to keep them in place not just with myself but with others, including family. About self sabotaging and how I can get out of my own head. How I can quiet the negative thoughts and focus on the positive. About anxiety and how I can calm it. All the techniques to push it away before it approaches at full speed. About breaking cycles. Finding my voice and my own independence. About narcissistic behaviors and how to notice some of their traits in people, including myself. About manipulation and gaslighting. About relationships and how I can control certain emotions not just about myself but with others. Guided me to notice my attachment styles and how I can do the work to heal those certain wounds. Remembering that I'm only able to control my own emotions, not others. That's on them. Stop people pleasing. It's helped me find ways to navigate through the waves of grief. It's helped me show grace towards myself in all areas of my life.

Therapy has opened my eyes to so much. It's helped me continue the work when I'm not in a session. I've read many books. Watched many YouTube videos. Listened to several podcasts. It's helped me go on my own self healing journey. It's also allowed me to find my voice. It's helped me find my truth. The truth. Share my experiences with the world. Share what I've learned for those looking for advice yet are scared. Therapy has changed me for the better and I'm forever grateful for going forward with it. It's opened my door to unlimited possibilities. Like writing this book and sharing my story with all to read. Hoping to help at least one person heal and find their voice.

It's even helped me understand and heal my attachment styles. I never knew the difference for each style or knew certain actions had a title. Learning and healing those have opened my eyes and mind up a lot. It's helped me understand every relationship I've been in and why actions were done the way they were from both parties. Therapy has been such an overwhelming yet fulfilling adventure. One I'm extremely proud of for myself!

If you are still debating if you should partake in therapy, I say do it. That's your internal world screaming at you to heal what was destroyed. It sounds scary yet it's completely safe. It may feel as if you're throwing in the towel for feeling defeated, but in reality, you're a winner for realizing you need it. Therapy is not a waste of time. I'm here to tell you that you're not weak for choosing better. You are actually pretty strong for taking that step.

14

CHAPTER

When it comes to concerts, I'm for the most part with friends. December 2019 would change that. It was the first time I ever attended a concert solo. If I can't find anyone to go with, I'll not go. I'll let others' decisions dictate mine.

One of my favorite bands, whom I've seen numerous times, was coming into town. I had asked a friend if they wanted to go. They had said yes. I bought the tickets. The week before the show this friend had canceled on me. I was stressed that week. Fighting with my internal voice of what I should do. Not go. Go. Sell the ticket. Go solo. Ask someone else even though not many people knew nor liked this band. My sister had to work that night of the show. I had no idea what I was going to do.

I finally decided a couple days before the show that I was just going to go solo. There's always a time for first times and this was going to be one of those times. As I'm getting ready that night, those silly anxiety nerves of "Am I making the right decision. Should I just not go since I have no one to go with. I'm going to look silly just standing there by myself…" decided to get ready with me. I told myself to just take a minute and take a deep breath. I'm not the only one who's doing this. There's been many people who go do things on their own. This is just the beginning for me.

As I got to the show to park my car, I felt a big rush of anxiousness come through my body. Like I was going to have a panic attack. I was about to go back home. I sat with myself for a bit. Took some more deep breaths with my hands like a butterfly wing on my chest, like my therapist had told me to do in situations like this one. Once I calmed down, I went into the marquee. As I'm standing there watching the opening act, the singer to the main band walks right by me. He's one of my favorites. Met him several times throughout the years. I had asked if I could get a picture with him. No anxiety was even present at that moment. I knew I had made the right decision after that picture was taken.

Throughout the concert, I had to stop and just soak in the moment. The moment that I actually let courage win. The moment that I did not let anxiety completely take over. If you know me, concerts are my safe place. My therapy. My zen. I absolutely love concerts. Been attending them since either 1999 or 2000. Can't fully remember. It's my escape from reality. I feel free for several hours. Like when I was younger on that swing. Best feeling.

That night was the beginning of what was to come later in life. It led me to travel out of state on my own to see another one of my favorite bands a few years later.

"Stepping out of my comfort zone and attending a concert solo is probably the best thing I could have done thus far in life. For some it's the norm, but for someone who's ALWAYS had people with them, it was dreadful… to say I'll do it again in the near future is not a lie! I love finding bits and pieces of me that I didn't know existed."

15

CHAPTER

2020 will forever be the slowest year of mankind. The year everyone will remember as one of the most chaotic years. The year the world shut down and time stood still thanks to the Covid-19 virus. It was truly one of the most interesting years of my life. Of your life as well. I'm still trying to heal from it.

For me, that's the year I lost not just my cousin, but my best friend of a cousin. She was my inspiration all throughout my life. She may have been younger than me, not by much, but she was my hero. Forever will be my hero. She had special needs. Cerebral Palsy. Epilepsy and other things. My main reason for wanting to help however I can in the Special Needs world. For her.

I remember the week leading up to her death like it was yesterday. I was having car issues. Family members were there to help me out. My very last resort. Felt a little guilty for asking once I found out their situation. Tried to find other ways around my situation so I didn't have to bother them this time yet nothing was working in my favor. I had told them to keep me updated and I'd do the same. Days go by and we get the message that my cousin has passed away. My heart broke and when I say it broke, it shattered into these very little tiny pieces. Like when you break glass and you're still finding pieces months later. Smaller than when all my other family members passed away. One of my best friends was gone. Just like that. Could not understand it saying when she was younger, she was told lies of when she'd pass away and she overcame those ages. Why couldn't she overcome this one?

The night I got the news, my childhood came and every memory I had with her came into action. Sitting at our grandmother's dinner table playing her favorite card games of Go Fish and the matching game with her. Playing Mario video games with her. Going to the park when younger on Saturday mornings with our grandmother. Every moment I got to spend with her those short 32 years of her life were right in front of me. It hurt my heart. It still does years later. She had this smile that would light up every room she walked into. She had this contagious laugh that would just heal your bad day within seconds. She just had this positive energy about her that would make that day's stress go away. I loved spending every moment with her as I got older. She was my hero in life along with our grandmother. Still today. This girl was the true definition of bravery, of strength, of love, of laughter, of light. I miss her every single day of my life. Hurts me knowing I didn't get to say those final words of "see you later!"

Since her death, I've distanced myself from my family. I've been healing on my own with this. I've tried to make it "better" yet I'd leave feeling worse than before. When I say this death hurts my heart, it really hurts my heart. I'm never going to hear those words of "Heather, is that you" as I walk through the door. I'm never going to hear "You're the girl I pick. I was looking for you." Those were her famous words when she saw me. That hug is deeply missed.

Since her death, I try to celebrate her life on her birthday and her anniversary any way I can. I try to keep her name alive. I always show my love for her on my social media accounts. That girl was truly one of a kind. Everyone needs to know how special she was to not just me but everyone that knew her.

This past June marked her fourth anniversary and my dedication is as follows:

"To the girl I pick,

These last 4 years have been different, that's for sure. I will forever search for moments of you. In the things you loved. In the color purple. In the places we went. In all of the movies we watched growing up. In all of the beautiful things that remain. I will always keep talking about you. You deserve to be remembered.

Until I see you again my beautiful cousin."

Even as I'm typing this chapter of my book, I'm getting teary eyed. I was debating if I wanted to share this part due to not being 100%. I heard this voice in my head of "go and share this part. She's a part of your story. She helped you grow as a woman. She helped build some of your character." My cousin may have been younger than me, but she showed me more in life than I could ever imagine. Her time may have been cut short but the time we did have together was truly the best 32 years of my life! I'm forever grateful for the bond we had growing up.

She was and still is my hero in life! I'll forever be the girl she picked because she's forever the girl I pick!

16
CHAPTER

With the world going crazy. Politics acting like unsupervised children. This virus taking us for an unpredictable ride. I knew I had to do something memorable for my birthday once again. I decided I was going to skydive. My introduction to 35 was going to be amazing. This time, I planned it all by myself. No financial help was needed from others. I've learned my lesson from previous times. With Covid-19 being in full force since March, I said screw it, I'm going to follow all the safety guidelines I need to in order for this to happen.

Wednesday, November 18, 2020, I FINALLY crossed off my number one bucket list dream and I went skydiving. It was the most incredible moment of my life thus far. Everything that was going on in my life was literally left out in the wind. I was free from it all. I even told my instructor as we're gliding through the sky that I needed to have a moment and just soak it all in. He respected my wishes. It felt as if I was a little girl again on the playground swinging. I was free. I wasn't thinking of all that has happened in life. It was the most amazing experience.

When people ask if I was nervous or scared, I tell them nope. The only thing that bugged me was the flight up to the dropping zone. Haha. It was taking forever to get up there. I was ready to go. As we were flying up to the drop zone, I did have to look around. Acknowledge the fact that I'm actually doing this. I've been wanting this since I was in high school and it's finally happening. I'm ready! I did have people confused on how I could do something so "terrifying" while having anxiety. No matter what I would do in my life that takes me out of my comfort zone, I'm always going to have that one person who just doesn't see how I could do such.

"...and with your anxiety, this would be the last thing I'd picture you doing. Even with a bucket list, you don't seem like the type that would have such a thing.."

Yes, I have anxiety. Yes it does get the best of me some days, but I'm not going to let it control my life. I'm not going to let it define me as an individual. Someone who does love the adrenaline rush. Someone who does love to have fun. Anxiety is just a lingering hair on my shirt that I can't find, that's all. It's not me.

Yes, I have a bucket list. Yes, I try my hardest to cross things off of it. May take me some time, like decades, but I get them accomplished. They get crossed off and dated. Just something I've had with me since I can remember. Yes, it does get changed up here and there, but it's always going to be there. My bucket list is for me. My own personal private goals. I don't share what's on that list. Yes, I get that weird look like it's just a list, but it's my list. I may show you the finished product, if my heart desires. Like this dream.

Having anxiety and a bucket list is who I am. I will not let this lingering hair be the setback of accomplishing my goals and dreams. I will not let it control my life and put up barriers to keep me from growing. From learning. From exploring. From achieving. I will continue living my life, one rush at a time!

Once I got on the ground with my feet feeling like jello due to the parachute straps, it finally hit me that I actually jumped out of a plane. I did what I said I'd eventually do. That car ride home was full of excitement. Fulfillment. Achievement. Proud. That car ride home with my sister was one I'll remember. Beyond grateful that she was there to witness it.

When I say that day was the introduction to 35, it was the introduction to what was in store for me and my challenge to step way out of my comfort zone on my following days of birth. It's led me to some amazing adventures. It's led me to some incredible moments of my life I did not know could exist. To say I love stepping out of my comfort zone would be one big understatement! It's become one of my favorite traits about myself!

17

CHAPTER

The night of April 3, 2021, is a night I do not wish upon anyone yet it's a part of someone else's story as well. It's not just the night I lost my grandfather Terry, my mother's dad. It's the night I made the decision to walk away from my family. This is a night I don't talk about much due to the hurt it's caused me. I've just now started talking about it fully in therapy. I'd share bits and pieces, but now it's the full story. I told myself I'd finally share it for all to hear due to possibly helping others understand trauma and what it can do to one's life. That it IS okay to walk away from situations that cause you harm, even if it is family. To me, that's just a word with so much meaning. We all use it differently and that's okay. Family is such a small word with so much meaning.

Once my grandfather moved away to Kansas the summer after I graduated high school, I did not talk to him as much. Not like other members of the family. They'd go and visit him. I'd call him here and there just to say hello and hope he's doing well. These phone calls only lasted no more than 5 minutes. He was the first person I called once I got my drivers license due to him always teasing me when I was going to get my license. It became our own little inside joke. So, of course once I got that tiny plastic card in my hand, he'd be the first to know. He wasn't much of a talker on the phone. Or was I saying the wrong conversation starters? I'll never know the true answer.

As the years went on, his health would decline. He'd have respiratory issues. He ended up moving back to Arizona. Just down the road from us. We hardly went over due to work schedules and other arrangements. Including 2020 and with us being out in the public. Didn't want to bring unnecessary germs into his house with his unstable health. Unlike others. Our conversations on the phone were still no more than 5 minutes. He kept the calls short and sweet. As long as we heard one another's voice, it was okay. So, I thought.

The night of his passing was probably one that could have been prevented yet I know we all suffer in our ways. Deal with grief in our own ways. Even today, I try to figure out where the words that were spoken to me and my sister came from with this individual. The one individual who I least expected it from in a way. These words that were not spoken TO us but ABOUT us to the one person who again was in her most vulnerable state. The one who just lost her father and had to find out through a phone call. These words were spoken to my mother in the same breath that shared the news of her dad passing. If that's not okay, I don't know what is. Still upsets me. Angers me. Why I've decided to fully talk about this ordeal out loud. With my therapist. It's time I regulate these emotions and heal the wound.

This certain individual took it upon themselves to call my mother and let her know about the passing of their father. In that same breath, they had told her that her daughters were the worst granddaughters. Yes, my sister and I were labeled "the worst granddaughters." Like I said, till this day, I'm still trying to figure out where those words came from with this individual. The one individual my family helped out numerous times growing up. The one individual who took advantage of my mother after my father passed away and helped themselves in my mothers apartment. Where was this coming from? And why? Is it because I'd talk about my other grandfather on my social media accounts? Is it because grandpa wasn't in the mood for company when we'd talk with him? Is it because we didn't go over and say our last "see you laters" when it was brought to our attention? What was it?

The next few days and weeks were such a blur. I was hurt by that. I did not want to see this individual nor talk with this person. They meant nothing to me. I was disgusted by it. Everything that was happening was showing me exactly why I needed to finally break free from these people. I remember breaking down in a kitchen explaining myself and how certain people will never understand what my sister and I had to go through with my grandfather Victor. Why we made the decision to not go and give our "see you later" speech to grandfather Terry. We were traumatized by what we experienced back in 2016. I remember I was speaking my mind that day in that kitchen. I can't tell you what exactly was said, but I do remember I was speaking my mind. That same day it was brought to my attention that other individuals were jealous of my posts I'd make talking about my other grandfather. Again, we all cope differently when it comes to grief and what not, but what's there to be jealous of? I respected grandpa Terry's wishes when he said he wasn't in the mood for visitors. I respected his choice to not talk much on the phone. With my other grandfather, I had to be there for him. I had to help him with things. What's there to be jealous of? That statement also stuck with me for quite some time.

Going to my grandfather's trailer to get some of my mother's things she had asked for was a little nerve wracking. Not knowing what to expect from people. While going through one of his drawers, I had come across a picture he had kept after all these years of me sitting on one of his little tractors from one of the tractor shows we went to. When I saw that, my heart broke. I did not break down. I sat and reflected back on that day. While in high school, my grandfather would invite me to some of these tractor shows. I'd say yes. It gave us some quality one on one time away from the other cousins. If he didn't invite me to go with him, he'd ask me to stay at my grandmother's house and "baby sit" her as he would joke. I loved those moments the most with them individually. Seeing that picture may have broken my heart but it healed my heart. He did cherish those moments just as much as I did.

When it came time to have his Celebration of Life, I was already in my "I don't want to be here around these people" mood, but I did it for my grandfather. I did it for my sister. So she wasn't alone. I did it for my mother who couldn't make it. I remember I took it upon myself to answer the front door. Sure enough, the individual who I did not want to interact with was standing before me. I felt a rush of anger flow through my body. They started to apologize and I quickly told them right now is not the time nor place. Till this day I have neither talked nor seen this individual along with others, which I'm perfectly okay with. This individual has tried making their way into my life via social media messages. I see them and quickly delete them. I have nothing to say to this human being.

After that day, I told myself I was going to walk away from these people and continue to heal more than ever. Heal what was taken from me. My worth. My voice. My dignity. It's been a couple of years now and in all honesty, I've been better since choosing to walk away. Your average person would not understand this decision because they're focused on that "family is everything" mentality and that's okay. We're not all the same, especially when you've been dealing with toxicity and trauma for so long.

I was asked by one of my therapists if I would ever be ready to talk with any of those people. My response to them was, not as of right now. Who knows, maybe later in life, but right now I'm fully committed to healing and keeping my peace of mind. My happiness yet again. My joy in life. If they can't fully accept and understand my decision, that's on them. Not me.

For those who've made the courageous move of walking away from family to focus on your peace of mind, I'm here to let you know you're not alone. Your decision is valid. Boundaries aren't meant to hurt you, they're meant to save you and your sanity!

Once my grandfather had passed, I of course, tried to keep his and our memories together alive. He was the one guy I looked up to growing up. Kind of like the "dad" figure. I found safety in him that I didn't find with my own father. This year, 2024, marked his 3rd anniversary and I took it upon myself to share on my social media accounts. In my journal as well. Boy, if only you could see those entries, you'd understand why I made the decision to walk away. You would understand why I keep his memory alive for all to see and read. I do it for healing purposes.

My grandfather Terry Johnson meant everything to me and on the night of April 3, 2021, that was taken from me. That night is now a part of my grieving story. Not how I envisioned how it'd go, but not everything in life is predictable.

"What's beautiful about life and family, we all have our own special memories with one another. Not one memory will be the same exact as the others.. And to me that's beautiful.

The memories I have with my grandfather will forever be something special. He showed me more than he knew. He taught me more than I can ever thank him for. He gave me so much in life.

Grandpa,

3 years has felt like forever but it has also felt like it all happened yesterday. That night replays over and over in my head. One night I honestly wish I would not play on repeat. Yet, that night led me to where I'm at now in my healing journey. It opened my eyes to so much around me and what I was allowing in. That night is a part of my story now and I'm forever grateful I turned something horrendous into something beautiful for myself. Thank you for everything you did for me. For all the beautiful memories we made together. Thank you for picking up the phone when I called YOU first after getting my license. Thank you for showing me the ropes in life. Your presence is greatly missed. Your sarcasm is forever carried on along with your blue eyes and dimples. I hope I've made you proud thus far in my life. I love you and miss you!"

18
CHAPTER

I've always found a love for traveling and I believe it all started when we'd go up north every winter as a family for the day. One of the few fun family adventures we'd all enjoy together. When everyone's moods were right. Even as an adult, I try to go up north in the winter for the day to play and see the snow. Just something that's stuck with me.

When I would travel as an adult, it had to be with friends or family. I guess you could say they were my comfort blanket. My security. Like when I was younger. My birthday weekend of 2021 changed everything.

Traveling solo always hyped up my anxious mind. I'd fall into the self sabotaging trap. If I wanted to go somewhere yet others couldn't, I'd stay back as well "wishing" I had gone anyways. I knew I wanted to step out of my comfort zone yet again for my birthday, but didn't want to do anything too extreme like my last one. I had always wanted to check out the Botanical Garden yet no one would go with me. Thought it was too boring. "Why pay to look at different plants when you could just look outside" is what I'd always be told. Haha. I also fell in love with the small town of Bisbee when I went there years prior with my sister. It's such a cute historic little gold mining town.

This birthday I decided I wasn't going to invite anyone with me. I was going to step out of my comfort zone yet again, with my therapist's help, and fight the anxiety bug. I bought my ticket to the Garden with no hesitation. When it came closer to that day, I would feel my body get anxious. Get nervous. The inner critic started kicking in. Self sabotaging was becoming heavy. I found myself journaling every night to quiet the voices. This was something that needed to be done. For me. This was something that I wanted to get done. I'm not going to let anxiety win. Never.

That Thursday morning of November 18th, I took myself to the Botanical Garden. To say I was anxious would be such a lie. I was extremely anxious. Alone at a place I've never been to. I don't know what I'm getting myself into. All the unnecessary thoughts were activated. I arrived early. Before the doors were even open. If it's one thing that will trigger my anxiety, it's being late. I am ALWAYS early, NEVER late! It's always been like that since high school. Before I even knew it meant anything. It's become a huge part of me and my planning. Haha.

When I got to the Garden, I felt myself getting overworked with anxiety. I found a bench outside the gates. Decided to sit on it and just let the nice crisp Fall air hit my face. Eyes closed. Calm my body. My therapist at the time was giving me tips and recommendations on how to calm my nervous system. Something I never knew existed. I didn't even know what the nervous system was. She had told me that sitting in nature, "grounding" will help calm it. So, I found myself sitting on that bench until the gates opened. Best technique till this day. Why I find being out in Mama Nature as I call it very zenful. When I say that the Botanical Garden is breathtaking, I'm not lying. It's filled with so much beauty. Who knew there were so many different types of cacti. And I'm an Arizona Native. I learned a lot about Mama Nature that day. Haha.

That night for my birthday, I got my closest friends together and we went out for dinner. As I'm getting older, I love having those close to me under one roof. At one table. I love that my tiny group of friends are so easy going. Mingle with everyone. Now that they know and remember each other. Haha. It was such a beautiful night. It was such a fun night.

Saturday morning, I took the drive down to Bisbee on my own. It's funny too because I remember that morning so clearly. Adele had just released her latest album. Me being a huge Adele fan, I of course bought it. As I'm getting on the highway, I find myself tearing up as her song is in the background (this is the first time I'm sharing THIS experience with the world). When I feel the tears coming down my cheek, I start laughing. "It's 5 o'clock in the morning. Who cries at 5 in the morning listening to Adele on the highway", I thought to myself. It then hit me that I was actually doing something huge in my life at the time all by myself. I was stepping out of that certain comfort zone. Those tears were tears of achievement. Tears of healing. Those were tears of finally fulfilling something I thought I'd never really do in life at that moment. Anxiety has its ways of holding moments back. This one was not being held hostage.

As I arrived in Bisbee, I was filled with excitement and safety. What people don't know of why I delayed traveling alone is due to the anxieties of being followed [I've been followed before, not on the road but in public], running out of gas, and something happening in the middle of nowhere with no signals. I still have these anxieties but they're not as controlling as before. So, that's why a sense of safety came over my body when I arrived.

I spent the day exploring the town. Saw some familiar spots from my last visit. Ate at a new place. Later to find out there's a few out here in the valley. Walked up their steep hills and stairs. Shopped at some of their antique stores. Bisbee has become my favorite little town in Arizona and there's many here.

As I was coming home, a sense of proudness ran through my body. A big ole smile came on my face. I felt like I accomplished the biggest achievement of my life at that moment. From someone who let driving anxiety take up so much of her life, THIS was a huge accomplishment. I was a woman FINALLY taking her own chances and challenging herself. Finally going on her very first solo road trip. To this day, that trip has become my favorite. It may sound silly to some, but for me, it was what needed to be done. It opened the door to many more solo road trips later in life.

19

CHAPTER

Christmas Eve 2021 was the start of my own holiday tradition. Since my Grandmother Judy's passing, Christmas Eve has been held at another family member's house. With everything that had happened lately in my life with the family, I took it upon myself to start my own tradition with boundaries and enjoy my own company. Heal those wounds that were caused by others. I now celebrate Christmas Eve solo and I'm completely satisfied with my decision.

I've been hurt too many times by these people, I'm no longer going to fake it to make it because they're my "family". I'm not that little girl that keeps the peace for others anymore. I have found my own peace and I'm not giving it up for others.

Some don't understand my decision and that's okay, they don't need to understand it. If they want to continue doing such, that's on them. I'm my own person who chooses differently.

I was asked by my therapist if I'm wanting them to reach out soon. If that would give me better clarity in this healing process. That was a question I wasn't ready for. Am I ready for them to reach out?

I honestly don't know. I feel I have more healing to do. They took a lot from me. So, at this moment, no I don't want them to reach out. I'd love for them to keep their distance as I'm keeping mine.

Christmas Eve 2021 was my first and not last Christmas Eve alone. I'm either sitting in my own peace with a pen in my hand or I'm planning an out of town trip to get away for the weekend. This first Christmas I sat with my emotions. Let them be validated. I sat with myself and reflected on what had occurred that year and the years before. I journaled, as usual..

"Here I sit on the couch listening to meditation music with my windows open listening to the rain fall…. By choice. My plan was to go up north to Prescott alone and adventure through its historic town, but I let the voices win this time and let my body rest. Since taking on this therapy journey, I've opened my eyes some. Which is what I wanted. I want to grow. Learn. Achieve. Going in, I knew it wasn't going to be easy, and I'm completely okay with that.

Tonight, I'm choosing to sit with myself and listen to myself. I wanna get to know myself more. Tonight, I'm choosing to step back and appreciate this given moment. If any of that makes sense, because it does to me. I'm actually okay just sitting here listening to the rain fall and meditation music play. Some may find it depressing, but it's truly letting me relax my thoughts and just enjoy the moment. Mindfulness wins!

I get it, my family is "worried" about me but in all honesty, I need to do this solo. Only I can change the negative thoughts. Yes, they can give encouragement, but it's not enough. I need to do this journey for me and just me. I'm not going to be stuck in the same mindframe as some. I need to get out and live, for me. I've seen enough of what they portray as "family" and I'm not okay with it. Let me figure this out on my own.

Whoa! That was random and probably doesn't make sense. Just thoughts running together.

This Christmas Eve was one that I wanted to do. Needed to do for me and my mental health. This Christmas Eve is my new tradition, maybe! Ha! I can remember all who left me too soon this way. I don't need to be sitting in a room full of other family members. Yes, it can be good for the soul and what not according to society, but right now, it's like this.

To my grandma Kathy and Judy. To my grandpa Victor and Terry. To my dad, John. To my cousin. To my great-grandmother Dryden and Opal. To my beautiful and handsome angels, thank you for showing me love. Showing me life. Happiness. Gratitude. Bravery. Sarcasm. Peace. Harmony.

Thank you for all that you have done for me the short times you all were here. Thank you for teaching me without even knowing it. Your legacy will carry on until the end of my time. To my beautiful and handsome angels, until we meet again!

Love, me"

This Christmas Eve gave me clarity. Gave me understanding. Gave me reassurance that I'm doing everything I need to in order to live a peaceful life. This Christmas Eve gave me everything I was missing all these years. I'm here to let you know, it is perfectly okay to start your own traditions. It's completely okay to spend time alone, especially on holidays. Do not let society tell you any different. If you need to step back from what once was to heal, take that step back and heal. Your decision is validated!

20

CHAPTER

December 2019 and November 2021 opened the door to what was about to happen in July 2022. Concerts and road trips are two of my favorite things. If you haven't already noticed. Haha! They just make me feel free!

I had seen that one of my favorite bands was going on tour. I saw they were coming here to Arizona, but I had already seen them here. I wanted to see them in a different scenery. I've always wanted to check out a show at Red Rocks Amphitheater in Colorado. I saw it was the weekend of Fourth of July. I had just got my vacation days for work. Took a couple days off. I went ahead and bought the tickets with no hesitation. With no second guessing, like I'd usually do. Until my next therapy session when I was telling my therapist what I had done. Haha. She was proud of me for not letting the inner voices think otherwise. After that session, I booked my hotel. On my next payday, I reserved my rental car. Doing all of this with no anxiety in sight was something that felt a little off. I was shocked it wasn't around saying I've yet traveled out of state, let alone 12 hours away by myself. It's as if I wanted it to be there. Weird feeling to say the least.

As the days started to approach, that's when anxiety and the anxious feeling started to approach my days. The inner voices of "you've never done such, all this could go wrong" would creep in. Thank god for understanding people in my life to calm the nerves. Morning of my road trip, I woke up like a little kid on Christmas morning waiting to open their gifts. I woke up feeling good. Ready to go. I left at 4 in the morning as my sister was headed to work. What people don't know is my location was on for my sister to see. I got a lot of concerned talks leading up to this trip due to being a woman, solo and away from friends/family. I am someone who is very self aware when they go out in public. No matter where I'm going. Thanks to previous events in my life.

Once I got into New Mexico, that's when I got nervous. It started to rain heavily in certain areas. I always get nervous driving in the rain. I'm from Arizona where it hardly ever rains or downpours. As I got into Colorado's mountains it'd rain some more, but this was as I call it, the "Hollywood" rain. Just pouring heavy non stop. My anxiety kicked in. I was extremely nervous due to the rental car's wipers not working properly. I was gripping that steering wheel so tight my palms were so red. Hard to see out the window. And here I am in the mountains. Talk about scary situations. I put myself in tourist mode fast. Driving a little under the speed limit. Staying in the right lane. Doing everything I can to remain calm. This lasted for the last hour of my trip. The last 100 miles of my trip. Pouring rain. Once I got to my hotel and parked, I sat in my car a little longer to collect my nerves before checking in.

The next day I woke up refreshed and ready to go. It was concert day! I got ready. Journaled before leaving to release my excited nerves. Headed to the small town of Morrison. Found a yummy pizza place. As I was leaving to head to the Amphitheater, I saw a little creek running behind the buildings. I took it upon myself to follow the little river and just soak it all in. Be present. Another thing my therapist had suggested I do in situations like this. Be more present. Something I'm still adjusting to, years later. That river was exactly what I needed at that moment. It's like a sign from the Universe. I'm a very spiritual person who looks for signs in just about everything I do and achieve.

Driving up to the amphitheater was so surreal. The mountains were so breathtaking. Scenery was so clean. Air was so crisp. Something I thought would stay on my bucket list for some more time. It didn't hit me til that night standing there watching one of my favorite bands. Once I got to the parking field, my mind was a little blown away. The concert didn't start for a couple of hours and there's already people in line and even tailgating. Yes, you read that right, these fans were tailgating beforehand. Haha. It was cool to witness. It's as if everyone knew everyone. Small town mountain feeling.

Standing in line was fun. Mingled with some people. There was this mother and daughter behind me. We started talking. Let it slip that I traveled solo from Arizona. She gracefully told me her name was Jenny and that she was a safe place if I needed anything. I had told her thank you and thanked the Universe for that sign. Jennifer, being my sister's name. We call her Jenny or Jen for short.

Walking into Red Rocks was so breathtaking. If you Google Red Rocks Amphitheater and select the "images" tab, those pictures do not do this place justice. Kinda like the Grand Canyon. It's a place you have to see in person at least once in your life. Breathtaking. The steps in Red Rocks are such a workout. Lunges are in full effect. I may be skinny but those steps were taking my breath away, literally. I was doing lunges just to get to my seat. Haha. There were already a lot of people inside, so I found the nearest less crowded spot. Once I got all comfortable, I took a brief moment to soak it all in. I could not believe I was sitting at Red Rocks. It was truly a magical moment. One I'm going to cherish till the end of time. One I hope to repeat in the future.

It took the band past their scheduled time to come on due to very high winds. Slightly expected due to being in high elevation. I'm used to concerts ending at the time this show started. My age was showing that night but I wasn't going anywhere. I was going to stay until I couldn't stay any more. Once the band came on, life was great! I was in my happy place. My therapy. I was living my best tourist life. Singing my lungs out. Dancing the night away.

That next day I just hung out at the hotel. Got some much needed rest. Found a good pizza place right by the hotel. Took it back and just recharged my body for my drive back home the next day. I reflected on what had just happened the night before and how I did this all on my own. I challenged myself yet again and fulfilled something off my bucket list yet again. I took that bet on myself and won.

"3:49 pm Colorado Time. 2:49 pm Arizona time.

Concert hangovers are real, wholly moly. Last night was incredible. Had a very fun time. Grant it, Dirty Heads came on at like 10:30 pm, weather was a factor, but I wasn't going anywhere. They only played for roughly 2 hours if that. Usual set time.

I met a couple of people in line who were the coolest. A mother named Jenny who was behind me in line was willing to give me her phone number just in case anything happened. A "safe place" as she called it. Very sweet of her. Complimented my hair and eyes, as a typical conversation starter would go with me and whomever, which is fine. She was sweet or so she seemed.

I also met a fella whose name was Nick. We sat next to one another the whole show. He was there with his group of buddies from California. He's a Cali native yet now lives in Colorado. We had civil conversations throughout the concert. Funny dude.

Universe, thank you for looking out after me this whole trip. Such a relief. A blessing in disguise. Letting me do my thing while showing me some signs along the way. Much appreciated. Please continue looking out after me as I head home tomorrow morning.

I'm still in awe that I went through with this. So beyond glad I did it! Red Rocks is such a beautiful amphitheater. The scenery is insane. Breathtaking to say the least. I highly recommend it! Who knows, I may come back in my life. If not, that's okay.

I just love crossing things off my bucket list. Love accomplishing my dreams. Stepping out of my comfort zone. Beautiful feeling. A lot has been learned about myself. Here's to many more adventures that lie ahead for me, Universe!

Until next time!"

My trip to Colorado only proved to me that I AM capable of accomplishing all that is in store for me from that day forward. I AM stronger than what I allow myself to be. This trip was just the beginning to all open road possibilities!

Stepping out of our comfort zones can be intimidating. Nerve wracking. Challenging ourselves can be scary. They both can be rewarding. Fulfilling. Courageous. If you are someone who wants to step out of that box of comfort yet second guess yourself and your thinking, I'm here to let you know that those feelings are completely validated. Ways to calm those nerves are quite simple. I've given some brief examples of how you can step out of your comfort zone.

Set some clear goals that will motivate you to reach those goals.

Say "yes" more often to new experiences outside of your daily routine.

Do something new every day. Tiny ordeals lead to bigger achievements.

Start small when you're facing your "fears." Your confidence will grow.

Keep learning about yourself and your "fears." Continuous learning builds confidence.

Here's to taking that bet on yourself and stepping way out of your comfort zone. You've got this. Promise!

20
CHAPTER

As a child, I always found hot air balloons fascinating. Every time I saw one in the sky, I'd wish I was in one just floating away in the sky. Flying away from whatever stress was activated as a child. Just to be one with the clouds. My birthday was approaching and I wanted to do something on my bucket list that left me with an adrenaline high. Researched places that offered hot air balloon rides. Found a good company, reasonable price as well. They offer sunrise and sunset flights, as they call them. I chose the sunrise, saying I'm such a morning person and that'd be a great way to start off level 37.

November 18, 2022, I crossed off yet another thing off my bucket list and I rode in a hot air balloon during sunrise. Beyond what I had ever imagined. Such a calming experience to endure. The only "stressful" part was getting into the basket as it's rising into the sky. That was the only "scary" part. The basket is on its side as we have to climb in while it's rising into the sky. Growing up you don't realize how big the basket really is. I stand 5'7" and that basket came up to my chest. It was a good descent size. As we're soaring in the air, I'm giving all my thanks and gratitude to the Universe for giving me that opportunity to do such in life. If it's one thing therapy has helped with is enhancing my gratitude. I've always been a positive, uplifting person, but some days, I even need those reminders.

The flight lasted for a good hour or so. Being in that basket healed the little girl who would swing on the swings during recess. It healed the little girl who spent her days outside. Riding in that balloon was what my inner child needed. What I found fascinating is there's really no designated landing spot. The balloon literally goes wherever the wind blows. Haha. The balloon does have a pilot who controls the heat to keep the balloon afloat in the air. There's also a van on the ground following the balloon. The pilot and driver communicate back and forth throughout the flight. We had landed in a very well constructed housing development. There were marking sticks everywhere. Concrete blocks everywhere. Pallets everywhere. We were legit landing in a construction zone. The workers were even looking at us like what was happening. Haha.

Another cool thing about this trip was learning the history of the hot air balloon and why after every flight they offer a champagne toast. With the sunrise flights, they offer either mimosas, orange juice, straight champagne or water. I took a mimosa of course! The reasoning behind the toast goes back to the two French brothers who invented the hot air balloon's first test landing. It was an interesting brief summary. Once the instructor was done with the speech, he asked if there were any special occasions on this flight. I, along with another lady, mentioned it was our birthday. We all did a toast in celebration of our birthday. As I was soaking in the moment, being present like my therapist had told me to try and do, a group of ladies from out of state were doing their own toast and invited me over. That was pretty kind of them. These women are from Texas and every year travel as a group to different states and do something completely out of their comfort zones. I had mentioned that I'm beginning to do such for myself. Especially on my birthday. These women were so kind and beautiful. Think about them often. Hoping they've accomplished so much off of their list.

That experience is one I'm wanting to do again, but a sunset flight. We all know Arizona has some of the best sunsets in the Southwest. Some day it will happen. Taking chances, betting on myself and stepping out of that comfort zone will forever be my way of living. This experience showed me just that. Fear and discomfort is something that does not exist in my life. Go on that adventure. Explore the impossible. Meet others who have the same way of living. It makes for great stories, like this one.

"Omg!! Riding in a hot air balloon was such a beautiful experience. Highly recommend it. Best zen if you ask me. Breathtaking! Had to zone out for a minute and just take it all in. So fun. And at the end, we made a toast. The story behind that is really cool. Everyone found out it was my birthday, so we all toasted to that. A group of ladies included me in their toast as well. Beautiful ladies! I'd do it again, but instead a sunset flight…"

That journal entry was pretty much my inner child talking. She was truly living her best life at that moment. The fact that I've been introduced to my internal world after years of not knowing about such has been very interesting to say the least. So much neglect was given to my inner human growing up, I love that I can acknowledge her and save her. Let her experience life. Let her experience joy. That journal entry was all my inner child talking and I would not change any of it.

22

CHAPTER

Once I became an adult, I found myself in the kitchen cooking Thanksgiving dinner for my sister and I. Along with mom when she was living with us. Growing up, mom did the cooking or we'd go over to grandma Judy's house. When my Grandpa Victor was alive, we'd go over to his house with something we'd pick up on the way, usually Jack in the Box. Healthy, I know. Haha. That way he wasn't alone. Same with Christmas Day. We'd go over and spend it with him. Loved those moments with him. Shared so many stories, stories I wish I could remember today.

Thanksgiving 2022 I had no desire to cook. It would just be my sister and I. I was done being the one to do everything for the most part. I wanted to go on a solo adventure. Page is another small town here in Northern Arizona that I've fallen in love with. I told Jen what I had wanted to do, she respectfully said go for it. So, I booked my hotel and spent Thanksgiving weekend to myself.

Anxiety would be a factor due to me traveling to a new city. Every thought that was with me during my Bisbee trip came back for this one. I already knew the tools to calm my mind this time around. As

I'm driving, I felt my body get extremely anxious. My palms started to get all sweaty. I started to feel tingles in my feet. My vision started to blur up some. I took it upon myself to find the next gas station and just sit with myself. Deep belly breathing was one huge technique I've taken with me no matter where I go. Positive affirmations are another. Repeating "I Am Safe" as many times as needed. This lasted for a brief moment, probably no longer than 5 minutes. Once I felt good to continue driving, I was back on the road. I arrived early to the hotel, as usual. That time gave me time to drive around. See what Page had to offer.

After checking in, I told myself to relax a bit. My body needed it after the ride up. Told myself to catch the sunset at Horseshoe Bend that night. It's been on my bucket list since visiting years prior to catch a sunset. Forgetting it was Thanksgiving weekend, I arrived at Horseshoe Bend and boy was it flooded with tourists from all over the world. Haha. Finding a good spot on the Bend was a little overwhelming. Crowded everywhere I turned. I ended up finding a good spot. Right next to an elderly couple who were the sweetest. That night's sunset was breathtaking. Sat with it. Embrace it. Thanked the Universe for what it had given me that day. Experiences and all. Horseshoe Bend has become a favorite of mine. I'm a lover of Arizona's creations.

Driving back from the Bend to the hotel, I started to think to myself if it wasn't for my commitment to start therapy and choose to heal, none of this would more than likely be happening. I'd still be stuck in my old habits of letting others' decisions affect mine as well. Again, taking that chance and betting on myself turned out to be the best feeling at that moment.

The next day, I had booked a tour for Lower Antelope Canyon. Something that has been on my bucket list since my 20s after seeing it as Wallpaper for Windows. Haha. Beforehand, I treated myself to a hole in the wall breakfast place. Had some good ole bacon and eggs crepes with hot cocoa. It was so delicious. I ended up arriving early for my tour. Like 30 minutes early. Which, it may sound crazy but in reality, I was able to get in with another tour once I got there. So, see, arriving early to places and being solo has its perks.

When I say that those Wallpaper pictures don't do the Canyon justice, I'm not kidding. That place is beyond magical. The canyons never stop. And the way the sunlight gets in some of those canyon slots, top notch! I had to stop midway due to just taking everything in. Being present. Grant it, it was crowded beyond crowded with tourists, it was still phenomenal. I met this family from Germany. Sweetest couple. And the guy giving us the tour knew his history. I know they have to but I think he truly educated himself extremely well for this job. Wish I knew stuff from that day. I would share some. The tour lasted a good 2 hours I would say due to the overload of tourists that day. Thanksgiving day.

The next day I drove home and the whole time I was reflecting on what I just experienced. Something so magical. That car ride home was also full of gratitude. I felt extremely blessed and proud of myself for overcoming so much within those last couple of years. Page, Arizona will forever hold a special place in my heart.

"These last 2 days have been so amazing. I can get the hang of these solo adventures. I'm at my happiest… well, these last 2 days put me in that state of mind. Exploring Page, Arizona has been so breathtaking. Such a magical city. So much to do. Not enough time. Will need to come back for sure.

Omg!! Antelope Canyon is stunning! No words for how incredible it truly is. Pictures do NOT do it justice. Everywhere I looked, there was beauty. Highly recommend it! So glad I took the chance and ran with it. It's not a once in a lifetime opportunity yet it's a once in a lifetime opportunity. Grateful!

I'm beyond glad I did this trip solo. Much needed. Finding more and more about myself is where I need to be in life. It's been fun! So many blessings have happened. I have my angels along for the ride with me. They're keeping me safe!

Tomorrow I drive back to town. Back to reality. That's fine. Just in time for more exciting adventures. I'm not going to stop exploring my limits and placing boundaries where they need to be. I've wasted so much time already. It's my time now.

Here's to many more solo adventures that await!"

23
CHAPTER

I knew this time for Christmas Eve I wanted to go somewhere I've yet been for that weekend. I didn't want to stay in. I wanted to be out with Mama Nature. I've always wanted to go to Prescott and explore that town, especially during the colder months due to possibly being covered in snow. I had told my sister that I was once again not doing the "traditional" Christmas Eve. She respected my decision. Told her I was going to take a trip up north to Prescott for the weekend.

Christmas Eve 2022 in Prescott was exactly what I needed for my soul at that time. With all the other huge accomplishments I was given that year, this was the perfect way to "close out" the year. My work was open Christmas Eve, I remember I got off way earlier than usual. I came home, got my bags and headed out to Prescott. Took me a good 2.5 hrs. I thought I was going to get caught in holiday traffic, but I was lucky. There wasn't that much traffic. Blessings.

Once I arrived at the hotel, which was on the street name, Heather Heights. Now, if that's not a sign I don't know what is. Haha. It was meant for me to be there that weekend. Still believe it til this day. I got all cozy in my huge room for one person. Had a balcony to sit on, which was perfect for me and my writing. Once I saw that, I had told myself to make it a priority to see the sunrise each morning. And I did just that, sat on the balcony each morning with a cup of hot cocoa and watched Mama Nature grace us with her beauty. I would even write in my journal each morning with my intentions and plans for the day.

That night, I took it upon myself to sit outside on the back patio of the hotel and just watch Mama Nature close out the day with such grace. I sat there and did a lot of reflecting. A lot of thinking. I sat there and just soaked in every ounce of fresh air. The crisp chilly air. I did feel it at one point in my body of achievement. I was doing yet another thing out of my comfort zone. I was yet again healing all that was taken from me in the past. I was yet again accomplishing something big in my eyes. At that moment, I told myself to disconnect from the outside world and just live for those next couple of days. Be present. Allow myself to get to know myself. Soak it all in.

Christmas eve day, I woke up to watch the sunrise on my balcony with a nice cup of hot cocoa and my journal. Wrote down my gratitude list and my intentions for the day. It was such a beautiful sunrise, my pictures do not do it justice. There was still snow on the ground and mountains. Such a peaceful scene to capture. That morning I decided to treat myself to some self love/self care and I ordered some room service. That was the first time EVER that I ordered food service. I know, I know. Crazy to believe, right?! Waffles, bacon, eggs and a side of fruit. It was so delicious. After breakfast, I googled some hiking trails nearby and found 2 different trails that seemed really fun. Christmas eve day I spent it out with Mama Nature and her beauty. Just like I wanted. What I needed. Watson Lake is such a beauty. It's on my "go back" list for sure. The boulders there are just incredible to witness. And the trail, beautiful. It wasn't too crowded like I thought it would be due to the holiday. After that, I made my way to another trail. Constellation Trail. That trail is yet another beauty.

Once I got to Constellation Trail, I felt my anxiety coming through. I did everything I could to calm it down. Told myself that I'm safe and everything is going to be okay. It's a beautiful day. There's snow on the ground. On the mountains. Everything is going to be just perfect. As I started this trail, I told myself as well to not rush. I have all day. It's a long trail with a lot of different trails. Soak it all in. The one anxiety voice that would not go away this whole time was, "you're new here. You don't know about this trail. You're going to take the wrong turn. You're going the wrong way.." those voices would not go away the whole time I was on this trail. I'd say half way up, I finally decided to just turn back around and head back to the car. I let the voices win that morning.

Once I got back to the car, I sat there looking around and told myself maybe next time. It was a weird moment for sure. Anxiety decided to stay with me most of my day up til that night. I'd do everything I knew to calm such yet nothing was fully working. Being present scared me. Sitting and watching the sunset wasn't perfect. My body would not stop sweating and having the tingling feeling. Once I got back into my room, I took a very deep breath and told myself that it's okay to feel what needs to be felt at this given moment. It is Christmas eve, a day that is still hard for me to process now that I'm on my own. A day that holds so many memories. Every feeling that is going through my mind and body at this given moment is valid. That moment of my trip was probably the roughest.

The next day was Christmas and I took it upon myself to have an easy day due to yesterday's hardships. I woke up and watched the sunrise yet again with a cup of hot cocoa. Mama Nature showed up so beautifully that morning. Glad I witnessed such. After that, I told myself to not rush into any huge plans, just go with whatever comes to mind. Googled some places nearby and found yet another lake to check out. Lynx Lake will forever hold a special place in my heart till this day. That lake saw the best of me, let's just say that. Halfway through the walk, I saw this bench that overlooks the lake. Took it upon myself to just sit and take in the scenery. The freshness of the air. A few minutes in, I realized my eyes were filling up with tears. At first I started to laugh at myself. Why am I crying at a lake? Then it hit me. Healing is just like grief, it comes in waves. Healing is not easy by any means. Those tears were tears of healing. Tears of achievement. Tears of accomplishment. Those were tears that needed to be shed and I did just that, let them roll down my face. Once I was ready to continue, I took every step back to the car with much gratitude. Every step hit me differently. Meant something more than just a hike around the lake.

That day meant more to me than anyone will ever understand. That whole weekend means so much to me till this day. It was one that needed to obviously happen.

The drive home was such a relief. Stopping for gas was the perfect ending of the trip. My total ending in my birth year, $19.85. Again, I'm a spiritual person who looks for signs and that was my sign. Along with the street name my hotel was on. Heather Heights and $19.85 were my signs that Prescott will forever hold special meaning to my healing story. My healing journey.

That drive home also let me reflect yet again of my driving anxiety and how I don't let it dictate my life. I don't let it control my way of living. The drive home let me reflect on my healing journey and how far I've come since then. I accomplished so much that year and this was just the topping to the cake. The perfect way to end out the year.

2022 was the year I learned so much about myself and my limits. The year I took so many bets on myself and won. The year that left so many doors open for what was to come.

24
CHAPTER

I'm usually NOT big on movie dates, but tonight, THIS date was needed. Getting out of that comfort zone of going to the movies solo has been a struggle for me. This past weekend, I said screw those damn voices and I took myself on a date to the movies tonight. I then sat on the hood of my car and watched the sunset. It was beautiful.

To those of you who go to the movies all the time solo, you've earned my respect. Tonight proved me wrong. It's truly NOT that bad. It's the negative voices that make it bad. It's the anxiety of people staring. People judging. It's just those demons trying to rule one's world. That's pretty much it!

To those of you who are wanting to take yourself out, I say do it. Now that I've done such, it's such a beautiful feeling. You're going to be so proud of yourself like I'm beyond proud of me. You've got this! Baby steps WILL win the race. Strength will succeed farther than you'll ever know. I believe in you!"

June 2023, at the age of 37, I finally went to the movie theater solo. Felt a little awkward at first but as I was sitting there, it felt as if I was at home watching tv. That awkward feeling went away. I didn't realize how many of my friends go to the movies alone ALL the time. It's their serenity. Their zen. Nothing but mad respect for them.

Once it was confirmed that The Little Mermaid was being turned into a live action film and the actress was not at all what everyone had thought she'd be, I knew I had to go see it. One, The Little Mermaid is my all time favorite Disney movie and two, it was already causing controversy due Ariel being played by a african-american actress. It took me a couple of weeks to finally convince myself to go solo. I was letting the inner critic win til I couldn't much longer. It was payday, I looked at my calendar to see if anything was coming up, saw it was empty and the rest is history. Bought the tickets for that night.

Once the movie was over, I got to my car as the sun was setting. I decided to just sit on the hood of my car and take in the sunset. It was that perfect golden color. Golden hour as some like to say. Perfect way to end such a perfect night. As I'm sitting there, I'm of course reflecting on what had just happened. Started to laugh at myself, yes out loud, alone in my car in the middle of a parking lot. Haha. I was laughing at myself due to the length of time it took me to FINALLY go to the movies all by myself. To finally achieve something that was a big anxiety trigger for me. A trigger due to being judged. Being stared at. Just like going to a big popular restaurant all by myself. Which I did that following month.

July 2023, I took myself out on a date to a crowded restaurant and treated myself to a paint class afterwards. Again, I'm usually NOT a dinner date type of person but this one was much needed. It was brought to my attention by my therapists, all of them, that I need to do more self-love activities to gain that confidence back. I need to start hanging out with myself. Loving myself. Getting to know myself. I figured why not test my anxiety while I'm at it.

I've always wanted to treat myself to a restaurant date yet I'd let "fear" win that battle. What if people judge me? Talk about me at their table. Label me. I always have that little judgmental voice in the back of my head. It's a trauma response due to all those years of being bullied. I'm always looking to see if people are talking about me. I'm also learning to not pay full attention to those people. I know who I am and know what I'm capable of doing. I don't need approval anymore.

I knew I wanted to also take a paint class. Those have been on my bucket list for awhile. I've done a couple but those were with friends, they were not alone, what I wanted. I went online, looked around for a class, found one I liked and signed up. I decided why not kill two birds with one stone and go to the restaurant before going to the paint class. For sure test the anxiety. Haha. Told Jen what I was doing and where I was going. She told me to have fun and be safe. I'm always telling her where I go and what I'm doing for safety. I am a woman doing things alone. Easy target, right?

I get to the restaurant and when I say it was crowded, it was crowded. I felt the anxiety try to creep in a bit. Took some deep breaths and told myself that "I am safe. I am strong. I am capable of doing the hard things." I repeated those affirmations to myself a couple of times. As I'm doing such, I'm holding my glass of cold water. If you didn't know, cold water stimulates the senses and activates the vagus nerve. It helps break the dissociative feelings. Grounds you. Why when I'm at work and I feel anxiety coming on, I'll go and wash my hands with the cold water. Let it run a bit. Sing the ABCs twice, if need be. As I'm holding my glass and sipping on the water, I notice my body start to calm down. As that's happening, I told myself to be present and alert. Stay off the phone and just take in the moment. Being on the phone will overstimulate your nerves. I was present. I took it all in. Challenged those jitters.

Once I was done at the restaurant, I made my way to the art class. I got there early, as usual, so I just gave myself a pep talk. Once inside, not one feeling of anxiety came through. Every lady in that class was so kind and welcoming. I wasn't the only solo adult in that room who was on the journey of healing and challenging themselves. There were quite a few women in that room who were doing the same thing I was. Made me feel so much at ease. Feel safe. Comfortable. Made me feel good that I'm not the only one on this journey. Felt empowered.

Once the class was over and I'm driving home, a sense of joy and happiness came through. It was a while since those feelings were felt. I embraced them and let them happen. I was also feeling proud. Proud of myself for not throwing in the towel at the restaurant. For going through with it all. I got home and went to bed with a full heart. That night was such a special moment in my journey. One of my proud moments, for sure.

Tonight, I took myself to a fancy-ish restaurant that was crowded [big anxiety set off] and then went to a paint class.

I've wanted to sign up for a paint class for awhile now, but I would let anxiety win with the whole "I don't have anyone to go with"... up till a couple weeks ago. Finally said screw it and just signed up. So glad I did!

I'm loving this whole dating myself thing. It's been interesting to say the least… in a good way though. My angels are looking out for me because I've met some amazing souls along this journey. Self-Love has become my favorite type of love!

You already know, I'm doing what I've wanted to do. May take me a while, but those goals and adventures are getting crushed. I've wasted so much time already, I can't waste what's left! I'm on this wonderful dating site that I'm not deactivating any time soon! Haha!

25

CHAPTER

For as long as I can remember, looking in a mirror has never been easy for me. I hate checking myself out. When I'm getting ready, washing my face, brushing my teeth, all those things that involve looking at my reflection, I try to hurry the process up. It goes back to childhood traumas of being bullied. It goes back to young adulthood traumas of being called every nasty word possible by the ones you thought cared for you. It goes back to every trauma I've been put through. My confidence was taken from me. My love for myself was taken from me. My worth was taken from me. Until last year when I came across this famous author and podcaster.

I started following her on social media a couple years back. When I decided to heal. She has this book out called The High 5 Habit and it's about high fiving yourself every morning in the mirror. She started a 7 day challenge as well for her viewers. I decided to participate in it. I knew it wasn't going to be easy for me. I knew it'd bring up memories from the past. I knew exactly what I was doing and what it'd bring to my table. Why I chose to do it. Challenge myself.

I decided I was going to high five myself every night for seven nights after I was done doing my nightly skin care routine I started a couple years back. Again, stepping out of my comfort zone and trying to get my confidence, love and worth back. Once I was done, I'd stand there looking at my reflection. The first night was the hardest. Not going to lie. I broke down and just cried. I stood in my bathroom and cried for the girl that had her confidence ripped right from her. For the little girl that felt she was never enough. I cried for the girl who needed the guidance from others yet was never guided. It was a rough high five, that's for sure.

As the nights went on, I felt my confidence boost some. It was such a beautiful feeling. One I never felt before. I know to some that sounds so bizarre, but for others who've been in my situation, knows exactly what I'm talking about. I got to thinking to myself, why not do a photoshoot based off of the growth I've gained while on this healing journey. Based on the love and confidence I've gained for myself since starting this journey. I contacted my friend, Susie, who I've known for years and who is also a photographer and told her my idea. She fell in love with the idea and agreed to do it. Her business page on IG is: photos.by.susie if you're looking for a photographer. Her work is by far my favorite and I'm not being biased at all. She listens to your ideas and works with those ideas. I feel so comfortable with her and trust her work.

October 2023, I had my very first solo photoshoot. It was a little intimidating at first due to never doing something like this before. I'm used to having people with me. I've done one with Jen and Malerie and then we did another one for our mom with Malerie's family. This was totally different. I wanted to do it out in the desert and near water, my two favorite Arizona things. Haha. As we were taking the pictures, I started to feel my confidence kick in. We spent a good hour or so out in the warm desert in a long sleeve dress. It was worth it though. The pictures turned out so dang good. I loved my choice of dress and destination, it all ended up colliding together.

Once I got in my car after the shoot, I looked in my visor mirror and just gave myself a big ole smile. A smile that held proudness. My body has been through so much and to come out on top, it was such a beautiful moment. One I find myself looking back on when I get down on myself. Body dysphoria is real when you've been beaten down for so long. I'm not perfect. I'm human. I'm human with more confidence and more love than before.

This high five technique still lives on in my journey. When I feel myself sinking, I'm always finding that silver lining to my day. Once it's found, I'll high five myself right before I head off to bed. Give myself the compassion it deserves. Give myself and body the love it deserves. Boost that confidence. Shoot, I did it tonight after brushing my teeth. Today was a rough day, I needed that reminder that I made it. It's just a rough moment, not a rough life. Showing myself compassion while on this journey has made my inner child feel beyond safe. She loves it!

"Goodbye to all that was holding me back all these years and hello to what I've gained, confidence being the big one.

Loving myself how I should was something I struggled with due to past traumas. I've FINALLY found the love I deserve and I'm not breaking up with it anytime soon. I'm not done yet. This is just the beginning of something magical!

I love myself fully. I am always enough!"

26

CHAPTER

Grief is such a little word with so much meaning. When you hear that word you automatically think of death. Of dying. Wanna hear a fun fact about grief? Are you ready for it? Grief is also mourning the loss of the living. Yep, you read that right. You can also grieve the living. Meaning, you are allowed to grieve the person you used to be if you're trying to do better. Trying to heal those wounds. You can grieve the people you have let go of from your life. You're allowed to grieve the friendships that ended unexpectedly. You're allowed to grieve these individuals. They've all meant something to you. They've all helped you build your character.

Grief is also a lifelong journey. It's not linear. It's always going to be there with you just at different speeds of life. One day you could be happy, having a great time full of laughter and the next you could be extremely sad crying your eyes out due to a memory that popped up. There's really no in between of grief. It's like that annoying crazy ex that won't leave you alone. Always stalking your social media accounts and showing up as a "suggested friend". Except, you can't block this page. You can't report this account. It's going to be there, watching every move.

There's no time limit for healing either. Both my grandmothers and great-grandmothers have been gone for 20 years or so and I still have my moments of wishing they were here. I'll hear a song on the radio and remember them. I'll drive by their old house and trailers and remember certain moments spent with them. It'll be 14 yrs this September for my dad and not a day goes by that I don't miss him. He may have not been the best father figure, but when he was present with us girls, he was a good father. We'd go to sporting events together. Races together. We'd spend the day up north together. He even coached my lil league softball team for 2 years when I was in grade school. Grief does not care what day of the week it is, it will show up however it pleases.

February 2, 2022 was a day in my grieving journey that needed to happen. Dad had already been gone for 12 years. When he passed we had him cremated. Because it happened so sudden/unexpected, we had the option to get him cremated if we donated his body. We did just that. Well, I thought to myself, why not make this birthday celebration special for him. One to remember. I mentioned to Jen that we should FINALLY spread some of dad's ashes on Grandpa Victor and Grandma Kathy's tombstone. "Reunite them". That'd be the first time for us both that we've seen someone's ashes. Boy, was that an experience to say the least. Haha.

Sprinkling the ashes on the tombstone tore me to pieces. It FINALLY hit me after 12 years at that time, that he was gone. That moment hit me harder than the night of his death. It was an experience I do not wish upon anyone yet we're all going to experience such in life at one point. Now every time we go and visit our grandparents, we bring some of dad's ashes and we sprinkle some of him on the tombstone. Still hard to do but it's our way of healing. It's my way of healing.

Christmas 2023, Jen and I decided to sprinkle some of Grandpa Terry's ashes on our great-grandparent's [his parents] tombstones. THAT broke me. The night of his death replayed in my head as I was doing it and as I was saying my little speech to him. That night of being called "the worst granddaughter" replayed in my head. It was painful yet calming knowing he's finally at peace with his parents and with his wife.

That same Chrismtas Eve, I wanted to bake cookies, just like I did with my Grandma Kathy when younger. It was my way of healing my inner child and keeping those memories alive. So, I baked cookies while listening to some Christmas music. When we went to the cemetery that next morning, Christmas morning, to visit our grandparents, I brought the cookies along with orange juice and shared them with my Rohleder clan. It was a beautiful morning!

Every time we visit my dad's parents, we make it a must to go and visit our Granny and her husband as well. I've never met my great-grandfather but when I'm there, I make it a must to acknowledge him and talk with him. Thank him for bringing our great-grandmother into our lives. She was such a beautiful soul.

It's been a few years since my cousin's passing and I'm nowhere near healed from it. I try to find my peace with it but when I do, I don't feel ready. She was truly my inspiration in life and to have it ripped from me without saying "see you later," that hurts my heart. Her favorite color was purple, so on her birthday or anniversary, I try to wear some sort of purple. When she appears in my dreams, the next morning I go to my journal and I write her a thank you letter. It's my way of remembering her. My way of healing. Will I ever be completely at peace, eventually, but right now, I'm struggling.

Grieving is different for everyone who is experiencing such. We all handle things differently. Some of us may not even go and visit our loved ones at their gravesite while others go every day. Some of us may have not been close to family members, so mourning their death is not in their daily schedule. It's all perfectly okay.

When I decided to walk away from my family to heal what was destroyed from me, I was grieving their "loss" for several weeks.

Every childhood memory with them came to play. Don't get me wrong, we had some beautiful memories when everyone was together. Laughter was carried all through the house. Those were the moments I was mourning the most.

When I walked away from my best friend since the 5th grade, I was grieving our time spent together. Again, we did have some fun times. It was always an adventure when we were together, that's for sure. There's days I miss her but when people grow and choose different paths, all we can do is wish them well! Hope for the best.

Grief is a part of me and my story now. I didn't expect it to show up at such a "young" age, but I'm glad it did. It's shaped me into the person I am today. It showed me how to live a life full of gratitude. Full of grace. Full of sense. It's helped me understand people a lot more. Be patient with the human kind.

For all of my grievers out there, be gentle with yourselves. This is a lifelong journey. Embrace those beautiful moments you had with whomever, even if it was your old self, embrace who you were. That version of you deserves the best as well. When those random moments come through your body, accept them. Sit with them. Let them come through. That's your body's way of healing and if you're a spiritual person, that's a way your loved ones or inner human comes through. It's a sign. I'd embrace the heck out of it! Feel it for whatever it is. Validate it.

27

CHAPTER

Trauma is one crazy thing we all will have. It's an emotional response to a terrible event, such as a crime. An accident. Abuse. Neglect. The death of a loved one. No trauma is smaller than the other, nor bigger than the other. Trauma is trauma!

It can affect our daily life when it comes to trusting people, maintaining relationships and even taking care of ourself. Trauma can also cause depression, lack of self-esteem, and anxiety. Some individuals may deny their history of trauma and resort to substance abuse to numb the pain. To create a false self image.

Trauma does not judge nor have a specific way of affecting people. It does not have a time frame of when it'll show up or not. You can be perfectly fine one day and then the next day a trigger will happen and it will bring up the traumatic event.

Every time I hear The Band Perry's song "If I Die Young", I go back to my dad's passing. I go back to that month after his passing. I go back to his Celebration of Life. Because of what it does to me when I hear it, I refuse to listen to it. I can't till this day. I'll switch the radio dial to another station or song.

Every time I drive down Main Street, I pass my grandfather's trailer. All 30 yrs worth of memories start to play in my head. Cleaning out the trailer comes to mind. I Wish I can go into that park one more time yet knowing I can't due to it being a gated community.

Driving down Val Vista Drive, passing my other grandfather's trailer every single day to work, I will randomly get the night of his death in my head. I will get a certain voice in my ear of being called "the worst granddaughter".

Trauma does not care when and where it'll show up. You can be in the best mood hanging with friends and then a song comes on, you drive down a certain road, or even see something that brings those traumatic events back up. It does not care. Just know as you're experiencing such that whatever emotion is being felt is 100% valid. Do not let society tell you that emotions are not valid. They are.

Wanna hear something interesting? Did you know our bodies hold our trauma? That saying "Our body keeps score" is completely true. Our nervous system goes through so much as well. Trauma does not mess around. It's a beast and if it's not taken care of, it can cause severe mental illness. Why healing is so important. Why therapy is very important. Helps on how to control, handle and relax those events.

If you are someone who is currently trying to heal and patch up those childhood trauma wounds, know that you are not alone and everything will be okay once again. Our trauma does not define who we are today. We as the individual we are right now is so much better than what happened to us. Our internal world is feeling seen and heard. We as the humans we are right now deserve to continue healing for that little internal human. They need it the most!

28

CHAPTER

Healing takes patience. Healing takes time. Healing is not linear. It is not cured overnight. As much as we who chose to heal our trauma and want it to be done within 48 hrs, it's not like that. As much as Hollywood makes it look "perfect", it's by far NOT perfect. It opens up so many trauma wounds from within. Healing takes time. A very long time.

Healing requires you to choose you and you only. Over and over. It requires you to be vulnerable. It requires you to be uncomfortable with emotions. It requires you to see things from another's perspective. Your internal world perspective. It requires you to be consistent with the work. Healing requires more than what people "expect."

Healing can trigger many different mental illnesses you didn't know existed from within. Like anxiety. Depression. Insomnia. Even suicide, shockingly. There are so many different types of tools to heal these illnesses. Therapy being a huge one. Therapy is nothing to be ashamed of. It's one of the best decisions I've made thus far in my life. Therapy has put my trauma into perspective. Therapy has given me so many different types of tools to regulate my nervous system during those "hard" days.

Therapy has helped me navigate through the healing process of grief. It's helped me understand the 5 steps of grief. Healing along with therapy has helped me recognize certain situations and how to cope with those situations today. It has given me the strength to walk away from situations that no longer serve me. Educated me with boundaries and what they truly do to one's healing process. Healing has brought out awareness. It has prepared me for what is to come with healing. Healing has given me that opportunity to rebuild. Take action. Get my voice back.

Therapy has helped me heal my mental health more than I could ever imagine. It's educated me on what anxiety is, what triggers it, how to navigate through it and what tools need to be used to calm it. Therapy has also helped me understand my nervous system. How to regulate it. Calm it and heal it.

My ways of healing vary. I'm a huge journal writer, so I journal my emotions. I'll journal letters to all my angels when grief comes over my body. I'll go for a walk and be present in nature when I'm feeling overwhelmed. Grounding technique suggested by my therapist has been super helpful. When it's cooler, I'll even go hiking. Healing techniques are different for everyone. What works for me, may not work for others.

For those of you who have chosen to heal, just know your decision is valid. Your emotions during this time are valid. You are not alone in this journey. I'm proud of you for taking that first step of recognizing you want to break those generational cycles and heal.

As I travel on this healing journey of calming my anxiety, embracing stepping out of my comfort zone, relaxing my nervous system for when traumatic events are triggered, I'm finding so much from within. I'm learning so much about who I am and who I want to be. My vision is finally 20/20. My voice is finally free. I'm not that young girl who was afraid to speak up to those who belittled her. Who bullied her. I'm no longer that young adult who falls for the emotionally unstable. The Narcissist. I'm no longer that young adult who lets people's assumptions fill her head. That's their own consumption.

I'm loving who I've become thus far. I feel my most beautiful right now. Not just in looks, but in personality, inside and out. I feel more alive than ever. More eager to see what the world has to offer me. Being "trapped" for so long took so much from me. I'm free and ready to get out of that comfort zone some more. I was never a gambler but this healing process has turned me into one. I love taking bets on myself. I learn more that way.

Finding my voice along the way has been such a beautiful blessing. It's given me purpose to advocate for the shaken. For the individuals who are still fighting those internal demons. It's given me my power back. It's given me the strength to tell my truth. Share my truth. Let others know they too can find their voice and speak their truth when the time is right.

Healing is such a beautiful yet imperfect journey that I'm forever grateful I chose to travel down and I'm not getting off this road any time soon. There's so much more to be explored. To be learned. I can't quit now.

29
CHAPTER

As I'm writing this last chapter, I look back on my progress from where I was to where I am right now, and all I can really say is "wow!" I've been through so much yet I've accomplished so much. My trauma has been my motivation. Those bullies pushed me to find my voice. My strength from within. Those bad relationships helped me understand who I did not want to be anymore. Grow up. Understand my emotions and how to regulate them. Walking away from family has shown me that not ALL families are perfect and that it is okay to walk away. Put boundaries in place. Focus on my own peace of mind rather than pettiness and selfishness.

My trauma has pushed me to go to therapy. Get the help I needed. If I did not start going to therapy, I honestly think I'd be knee deep in the dark hole of life. Gasping for air. Therapy has helped me in more ways than one. It's helped me understand anxiety. It's helped me understand so much about healing. About grief. My trauma has motivated me to get out of that comfort zone. Take bets on myself.

When I say it's my motivation, it's my motivation to grow. Accept what was yet to focus on what is and what will be. It's my motivation to succeed in life. Share my story. My trauma is my motivation to continue healing my internal human. She deserves it the most. It not just motivates me but allows me to recognize and take full accountability of how I react to triggers.

I am at a place in my life where I'm truly satisfied with what I have done thus far. I have found my voice. My truth has been spoken. I continue to go to therapy. I'm taking more bets on myself than I ever thought I would. My gratitude jar is overflowing at the moment. I've found so much love and respect for myself. Life at the moment is what I've envisioned for quite some time. I'm going to embrace it! Hold onto it. Be present with it!

For my fellow healers who are trying to get there, please do not give up on yourself. Your gratitude jar will be overflowing as well. I'm here to let you know it is possible. Your presence is far more important than what those internal demons are telling you! You are Enough. You are Valid. You are Loved.

Acknowledgments

To my mother, Jo and my sister, Jennifer, thank you! You both have shown me so much throughout life. Jennifer, you're truly one of a kind. Best sister ever! Thank you for everything. You ladies have guided me towards better without even being my tour guide. Thank you and I love you both long time!

To my father, John, thank you for all those wonderful memories we shared growing up. Thank you for showing me more than I could ever be shown throughout life. I've taken it all with a grain of sugar and carried it into my own life. Your name is forever spoken. Not a day goes by that we don't mention it. Thank you for showing me signs when needed. I hope I've made you proud these last 14 years.

Malerie, my sister from another mother, thank you for your life long friendship. Thank you for being there during some of my most critical times. Your friendship means everything and then some. You've shown me more than I could have ever imagined. Your words of truth linger like that annoying piece of hair we could never find. They're forever a part of me now. I love you long time!

Grandma Judy, my forever angel, my hero. Thank you for everything you ever did for me. For my family. Thank you for being my safe place. My escape from what was going on at home. At school. Thank you for pushing me to do better. Be better. There's not a day that goes by where I don't mention your name. Where I don't talk to you. Where I don't ask you to show up when needed. You are greatly missed and I am forever blessed that I had you as a grandmother. I hope I've made you proud thus far in life. Your wisdom plays in my ear constantly.

Grandma Kathy, where do I begin? Your gentleness is missed tremendously. Thank you for being the grandmother you were. Those moments of baking in your kitchen every Christmas is cherished today. I hope I've made you proud thus far in my life. I wish we got more time together but the time that was given was truly the best. I love and miss you a lot!

Grandpa Terry, thank you for everything you did for not just me but my family. It truly meant the world at that time. Forever grateful. Thank you for showing me how to not take life so seriously. Sarcasm is not a bad thing. Thank you for choosing me to go to the tractor shows with you, that was everything. Beautiful memories today. I hope I have made you proud thus far in life. Your words of wisdom come through at the most perfect time. I love and miss you more than you know!

Grandpa Victor, oh man, you are missed more than I can ever explain. Every time I look up at the fireplace, I see your hat and it brings back so many wonderful memories from when I was younger. Thank you for acknowledging my voice that day in the hospital room. That meant everything. You taught me so much without even knowing you were teaching me. I love you and hope everything I've accomplished in life has made you proud.

To my beautiful cousin, my forever hero in life, not enough words could sum up the gratitude I have for you and our cousin bond. It was something I'm going to forever cherish. Thank you for changing me and how I see life. Thank you for showing me what strength, what love, what bravery, what courage looks like. Thank you for choosing me as your person because you're forever mine. I love you more than you'll ever know. Thank you for giving me the best 32 years of life with you!

Grandma Dryden and Granny, you two ladies were the true definition of beauty. Of class. Thank you for showing me grace. You two were such delights to be around. You both taught me so much about life at such a young age. Granny, you showed me that it's perfectly okay to get out of that comfort zone. Embrace the challenge. Grandma Dryden, you showed me love. You showed me peace. I love you both so very much. Beyond grateful for the time I was able to spend with you both. I hope I've made you both proud thus far in my adventure of life.

Nicole, thank you for all these wonderful years of your friendship. Of your shoulder to cry on/lean on. Thank you for being the best concert buddy. I love singing on the top of my lungs with you. It's the best! Thank you for your endless reminders of how life will be now that we're both in our healing era! I got you, girl. Love you long time!

Susie, I'm so grateful to have you in my life after all these years as my go to person for family or even solo portraits. Who knew two young adults at the time working at the same Childcare center would be good friends years later?! Thank you for listening to my silly yet creative ideas and going with them when it comes to portraits. That means a lot. Most importantly, thank you for agreeing to do my solo photoshoot. You saw me in my most vulnerable state and made me feel at ease during the shoot. I appreciate you more than you know!

Gina, girl, if it wasn't for you going to therapy and pushing me to go, I don't know where I'd be today. That's the truth! Thank you for guiding me in the right direction, the best direction of life. Thank you for helping me find my second job, even though you left me. Haha! Again, I don't know where I'd be in life if it wasn't for you and your push to do better! So grateful for our friendship, years later! You're truly an amazing person. Appreciate you long time!

About The Author

Heather is a Arizona native. Born and raised in Mesa where she is currently residing. She's a full time childcare professional for the past 20 years and a part time caregiver for the Special Needs community. She's had a creative soul since childhood. From painting, drawing to writing. Always found a safe place in writing. An avid journal writer since the age of 13. This will be her very first book ever released for all to read. This book has inspired her to continue the path of writing, hoping to release more books in the future. Continue being the voice for the shaken.